Are you sim~~ ~~ ...paigns to satisfy your own ego? That's what most companies do even though high ...ated tools exist to help you reach individual buyers directly with information they appreciate. *Precision Marketing* is your guide to creating relevance to your buyers and driving success for your business. **David Meerman Scott, international best-selling author of *The New Rules of Marketing and PR***

Marketers run the gauntlet of business every day. Saddle up; it's time for change! *Precision Marketing* is a great read! **Jeffrey Hayzlett, Marketing Maverick and best-selling author of *The Mirror Test* and *Running the Gauntlet***

Precision Marketing produces results. As a technology company, Ricoh understand first-hand the value of moving beyond print, integrating across multi-channels and leveraging data-driven customer insights. This book offers a perfect, proven and pragmatic guide to improving your business results. **Yasuhiko (Sam) Hosoe, GM, Global Marketing, Ricoh Production Printing Group, Ricoh Company LTD**

Today's marketers can't survive without developing valuable, compelling and relevant content to customers at the right time. *Precision Marketing* uses some of the best research on the planet to show you why, and how to leverage the right information to substantially grow your business. Read this book... then give it to your CEO. **Joe Pulizzi, Founder, Content Marketing Institute and best-selling author of *Get Content, Get Customers***

Powerful! This book is a real-world account of becoming a social business through the use of data to drive customer engagement. Read this book if you are a business leader who wants to be set apart and deliver improved results. **Sandy Carter, IBM Vice President Social Business Evangelism**

If you read only one book on marketing this year, *Precision Marketing* stands alone as the obvious choice. **Aaron Harber, CEO, American Research Corporation**

Zoratti and Gallagher describe Precision Marketing as a journey. In the diaspora that is marketing today, this book is a GPS for the professional seeking the promised land of high performance. Mapping ever more relevant programs that drive results just got easier. **John Favalo, Managing Partner, Eric Mower + Associates Group B2B**

The global marketing picture is shifting and changing daily. Zoratti and Gallagher present a compelling argument for shifting to a data-driven, customer-centered approach that stops focusing on the newest channel, but gets marketing back to owning the business driving experience. **Charles Lawrence, General Manager & VP of Marketing, Franke**

Today's marketers need to connect with tomorrow's customer in a new and intimate way to better segment and predict their behaviors. Zoratti and Gallagher illustrate this ever-changing environment through their 'Relevancy Era' by providing pertinent case study examples and recommendations on how to measure and optimize marketing practices to meet customer demand. **Jeffrey Boorjian, Vice President of Marketing, Caesars Entertainment**

The first Precision Marketing Moment is get this book, it is a wake-up call to marketers. Read the book and heed the advice to partner with your management team and really know your customers to win. **Al Maag, Chief Communications Officer, Avnet and Chair Business Marketing Association**

Being relevant in a sea of marketing messages has never been more important. Zoratti and Gallagher offer actionable insights on how to use data to engage buyers, drive revenue and avoid becoming irrelevant and potentially obsolete. **Mark Wilson, Senior Vice President, Corporate and Field Marketing, Sybase**

Precision Marketing addresses how to overcome marketing's relevancy crisis and offers actionable insights underpinned with market research and case studies on how to become more relevant to the only constituency that counts, your customer! **Martyn Etherington, Vice President Marketing, Tektronix/Danaher**

This book really gets down to it – it actually shows you how brands have won with Precision Marketing. Think of it as a 'How To' guide for tomorrow's marketer. **Shelley Kalfas, SVP, Marketing, Sodexo**

Precision Marketing isn't an unattainable theory – it can be done. You can lead with customer data to deliver a relevant experience. Zoratti and Gallagher not only make the case for relevant engagements that can drive loyalty, but back it up with roadmaps, examples and action plans that turn loyal customers into true advocates that can help drive revenue and results through advocacy. **David Roman, Chief Marketing Officer & SVP, Lenovo**

One of the great challenges marketers face is knowing and understanding the needs and expectations of their unique customer. The authors have not only clarified how to address this challenge, but have outlined what our peers have done to achieve meaningful success by adopting and applying the Precision Marketing mindset to their brands. **Eileen Zicchino, Chief Marketing Officer, J.P. Morgan Treasury Services**

Customers are not waiting around for brands to build relevant experiences. Marketers can't afford to figure out how to deliver these experiences tomorrow – this book helps identify the strategies that can be built today based on the best practices of global brands who have won with Precision Marketing. **Robin Korman, SVP, Loyalty Marketing & Strategic Partnerships, Wyndham Hotel Group**

Customers live in an always-on world filled with high expectations and demands. Marketers must exceed those expectations with solid experiences and business driving engagements... and there isn't time to waste. Zoratti and Gallagher offer *Precision Marketing* – a proven, practical mix of insight, action and measurement – as a path to build a winning global brand now. **Chris Hummel, Chief Marketing Officer, Siemens Enterprise Communications**

Data and insights about our customers, our markets and our brands are everywhere, and it can be overwhelming. But Zoratti and Gallagher lay out a plan for Marketers to start with whatever assets they have today... not tomorrow when customers have already moved on to other experiences. This book is a must for those marketers looking to take that next step and lead with insights and win with Precision! **Kim M Sharan, President, Financial Planning and Wealth Strategies & Chief Marketing Officer, Ameriprise Financial**

Zoratti and Gallagher point out why marketers may be their own worst enemy. This book spotlights why relevancy matters, how companies are making the shift and what the new benchmarks for success look like based on Precision Marketing. **Carla Johnson, Principal, Type A Communications**

Zoratti and Gallagher deftly articulate what many of us in the marketing community have been observing over the past several years. Now more than ever, a company's reputation – and bottom line – depend on its ability to deliver an effective and meaningful message to the modern consumer. **Michael Babikian, Senior Vice President and Chief Marketing Officer, Transamerica Insurance & Investment Group**

Forget mass marketing. Forget market segmentation. Precision marketing is the future, and Zoratti and Gallagher map a clear path to implementation. *Precision Marketing* is an essential read for marketers who want to survive and prosper in the 21st century. **Roger Dooley, author of *Brainfluence***

With the advent of social media, customers more than ever before vote with their immediate attention and share-of-wallet. The mantra of true cross-channel communication and marketing mix needs to come true, sending compelling and consistent messages, based upon real-time customer insights across all marketing activities. Sandra Zoratti and Lee Gallagher provide true evidence that the insight generation and actions provide real value, based upon compelling case studies. As the case studies clearly point out, the 'Relevance Era' in marketing will have multiple implications for using modern IT, different skills and competencies in marketing as well as driving the marketing organization to be the spearhead for establishing a true 'market-focused organization'. A clear must-read for all marketing and sales professionals. **Dr Ralf E Strauss, SVP, Head of Sales & Marketing Projects, Volkswagen Group, Wolfsburg Germany**

Precision Marketing

Maximizing revenue through relevance

Sandra Zoratti
and
Lee Gallagher

KoganPage

LONDON PHILADELPHIA NEW DELHI

First published in Great Britain and the United States in 2012 by Kogan Page Limited

120 Pentonville Road	1518 Walnut Street, Suite 1100	4737/23 Ansari Road
London N1 9JN	Philadelphia PA 19102	Daryaganj
United Kingdom	USA	New Delhi 110002
www.koganpage.com		India

© Sandra Zoratti and Lee Gallagher, 2012

The rights of Sandra Zoratti and Lee Gallagher to be identified as the authors of this work has been asserted by them in accordance with the Copyright, Designs and Patents Act 1988.

ISBN   978 0 7494 6535 3
E-ISBN   978 0 7494 6536 0

British Library Cataloguing-in-Publication Data

A CIP record for this book is available from the British Library.

Library of Congress Cataloging-in-Publication Data

Zoratti, Sandra.
   Precision marketing : maximizing revenue through relevance / Sandra Zoratti, Lee Gallagher.
      p. cm.
   Includes index.
   ISBN 978-0-7494-6535-3 – ISBN 978-0-7494-6536-0 (ebook)   1. Target marketing.
2. Consumer behavior.   3. Market segmentation.   4. Marketing.   I. Gallagher, Lee.   II. Title.
   HF5415.127.Z67 2012
   658.8′02–dc23

Typeset by Graphicraft Ltd, Hong Kong
Printed and bound in India by Replika Press Pvt Ltd

CONTENTS

FOREWORD

Generating positive marketing results isn't easy, especially in a challenging economy. Yet today's most impressive marketers have learned how to build their business and perform effectively in today's constrained environment.

Many of the strongest performers in business today have one thing in common: they've committed themselves to customer-focused strategies grounded in rigorous customer insight achieved through data mining, analysis and enriched profiling using third-party data sources, as well as behavioural, transactional and conversational tracking.

As Sandra Zoratti and Lee Gallagher pointedly explain, today's top marketers are engaged in Precision Marketing. Rather than devote marketing budgets to mass campaigns that treat every recipient in the same manner, Precision Marketers are mining customer data for predispositions and propensities to spend in order to target buyers in exceptionally sophisticated ways so that all communications are targeted and relevant to each and every individual recipient. The level of customer affinity and business results produced by these marketers and companies speak for themselves.

As the CMO (Chief Marketing Officer) Council's research demonstrates, some of the biggest challenges for today's marketers lie in engaging consumers in a more relevant and customized fashion. Only by reaching customers as individuals and using each customer's unique preferences and priorities, will we, as marketers, be able to build dynamic, profitable and lasting relationships. Using Precision Marketing methodologies, marketers will be able to cut through the clutter and turn their customers into full-throated advocates.

Marketers are recognizing that increasing customization and precision are critical to their success. In one recent survey of CMOs, nearly 60 per cent said they are focused on reaching their buyers in more relevant and contextual ways. These CMOs state they are now focusing on targeting, profiling and segmenting their customers to gain a better understanding of their inclinations and motivations, which will enable more effective and engaging communication.

The trouble? Marketers are only now beginning to generate sufficient amounts of customer insight to engage their buyers intelligently. Only 15 per cent of marketers believe their companies are doing an extremely good job of integrating disparate customer data sources and repositories. This cannot last. Success in the future will depend on the marketer's ability to launch initiatives that make customer data analysis and insight generation a top priority. It's time now to begin to focus on the data.

There is a growing awareness of the importance of data and the actions marketers must take to drive customer communication to the next level. As a result, and not a moment too soon, the Precision Marketing movement is gathering momentum.

Sandra and Lee are pioneers in this paradigm shift. With this book, they offer much-needed thought leadership on the power of Precision Marketing and the impressive returns associated with engaging customers as individuals. Through far-reaching analysis and compelling case studies, Sandra and Lee light a path to guide marketers in the coming years. As consultants to some of today's most recognized companies, they understand that relevance is critical to success – not just relevant messaging and communication, but relevant offers, deals and value-added solutions as well.

In this compelling book the authors have laid out a plan to guide you through the barriers that must be overcome to put a Precision Marketing programme in place. They have captured insights into some of today's most impressive enterprises, among them companies like Harrah's, Tesco and ING Group. Sandra and Lee bring to life their own experiences and lay the groundwork for your future success.

The Zoratti–Gallagher team make implementing Precision Marketing practices a can-do proposition by providing actionable, real-world advice that marketers can begin applying today. They show readers the challenges that must be addressed, the gaps that must be closed and the opportunities to be gained when launching an effective programme. As they see it, you already have available data, so you can start now. That's their key point: *get started*. Once you get rolling, you can test and learn, refine and expand.

Sandra and Lee clearly understand and outline the business implications associated with Precision Marketing – and lay those out in comprehensive detail. They point out, in no uncertain terms, that there are positive business and career implications for marketers moving in the data-driven direction. Sandra and Lee explain how the demand for increasing rigour and discipline is transforming the marketing profession and creating new routes to revenue and professional advancement. They show how marketers can add more business value by transforming customer data into customer insight to develop customer-driven businesses and high-impact customer-centric campaigns, interactions and experiences.

Further, the authors make the case that tomorrow's chief marketing officers and, increasingly, chief executive officers are likely to come from a background that emphasizes customer data analytics and insight. That's quite a change from the career paths of marketers in the past, who often tended toward brand-building and marcom-related activities. Even in the product realm, marketers were often buried deep in niches that put little focus on customer data and analysis.

That's all changing. Businesses can't win in today's hyper-competitive markets without knowing their buyers and prospects intimately – giving them what they want and anticipating what they will want next.

Companies are now expected to enhance customer value, strengthen loyalty and provide memorable experiences that truly engage customers. However, none of this can happen without deep customer insight and the ability to act on it. Enterprises that invest in these capabilities will out-manoeuvre their rivals and produce superior business results. These forward-thinking companies will produce far greater returns on their marketing investments. They also will create a culture and discipline for marketers and line-of-business leaders to build more enduring and robust relationships with customers.

Precision Marketers are now discovering the hidden gold that lies within customer intelligence. While the world may appear one way, appearances can be deceptive. That's why analysis and insight are so necessary. Our experiences and intuitions too often fail us in today's turbulent and fast-changing markets. We have to stay focused on our customers – and our prospects – if we hope to grow these relationships. Marketers must track customer attitudes and behaviours as those assets move through various life stages. Marketers need to know which customers are most profitable and which ones are most promising. By examining such factors with diligence and care, we discover our greatest growth opportunities.

This book will help you seize new opportunities. It offers an impressive makeover for your marketing organization, basing your actions in customer data and embracing the fundamentals of Precision Marketing. It offers a framework and game plan to drive your enterprise's success. You will learn the path to personal prosperity and professional growth that is yours to take. What could be more relevant than that?

Donovan Neale-May
Founder and Executive Director,
Chief Marketing Officer (CMO) Council

ACKNOWLEDGEMENTS

Every noble work is at first impossible. THOMAS CARLYLE

From Sandra and Lee:

Impossibility creates possibility. When faced with some daunting challenges in the world economy, warp-speed changes in marketing and a morphing business landscape, it was time to get busy creating the possible from the seemingly impossible. Thus, Precision Marketing was born. Finding ways to break through the cacophony that has become marketing messaging today, to stand out and to engage customers on a higher level – as measured by revenue and ROI – became our passion. The Precision Marketing team set out to create more value for our customers and for our business. We decided to hypothesize, test and prove in statistically sound ways and in metrics which the boardroom cares about. The results astounded us. In each implementation of Precision Marketing across a multitude of industries, applications and channels, we produced a minimum two-digit improvement in results over the status quo. Our first proof point generating a three-digit ROI was conducted the week that Lehman Brothers crashed. Wow. At that moment in time, we knew we had the foundation on which to build something transformational and amazing.

Our breadth of positive and compelling results spurred us to write this book and share our stories, experiences and metrics. Sharing our journey through this book is our quest to genuinely help others by learning from our walk. And marketers are under intense pressure to learn new ways, make a bigger difference and deliver stronger, measurable results. In our view, marketing is undergoing the most significant transformation of our lifetime andwe strongly believe that Precision Marketing's Moment is now.

From Sandra:

Thank you seems like such an inadequate expression of the gratitude to so many who contributed to make this book possible – from our customers to our colleagues to our partners and our friends. The four person team who worked most closely on this book is like my extended family and my gratitude goes to my extremely talented and creative co-author, Lee Gallagher, our incredible friend and project manager, Jean Marie Martini and our amazing friend and researcher, editor and supporter, Amanda Thall. Thanks, thanks and thanks. The CMO Council – a trusted and brilliant partner – was instrumental in helping to generate research and guidance in many areas that illuminated our path forward and helped us to clearly understand the voice of the marketer. Jeff Paterra, my manager, was unique in challenging the status quo and supporting the creation and publication of this book. Thank you, Jeff. To my reader goes my enormous gratitude, for your faith and support of this book and the premise and practice of Precision Marketing. My hope is that this book will inspire you, challenge you, encourage you and change you in a positive and sustainable way.

Woven throughout this book are parts and pieces of me. For who I am through their consistent and loving support and unshakeable integrity, giving hearts and a close family environment, I thank my parents, Josephine and Robert Zoratti, my sisters Deb Plewacki and Renee Rini along with Duane, Lauren, Derek and Nick Plewacki. You make everything possible.

From Lee:

Most of my career at IBM has been dedicated to selling complex solutions to the top Fortune 100 companies. I quickly determined that a good sales-person is constantly working and planning on how to exceed their sales quota but a great sales person has a selling 'framework' that can deliver remarkable, consistent results, year after year. For over ten years, my strategy and execution enabled me to be one of the IBM's top sales representatives, winning every sales award offered by the company.

After ten years of selling, my company offered me an interesting proposition – to move into a marketing role in order to replicate my field successes. I began to apply my selling 'framework' to my marketing efforts, following a best practices approach with a laser focus on data and measurement, eliminating any guess work. In time, enabling a strategy was able to deliver consistent results yielding great returns for both our company and our customers.

In 2009, Sandra Zoratti enlisted me as a data driven marketing advocate and suggested we co-author a book that would help other marketers deliver consistent, measureable results with rock solid ROI. From that conversation to now, our team has conducted 100's of interviews with top marketers and conducted countless hours of research over the past four years in the development of this book. I hope you will find this book insightful and the case studies valuable benchmarks to support your Precision Marketing efforts.

I thank Sandra for her guidance, fortitude and dedication to the creation and now completion of this book. To the team, especially Jean Marie and Amanda, a heartfelt thank you. And lastly, to my Dad who taught me from childhood that strategizing, planning, and hard work is what defines character and success.

ABOUT THE AUTHORS

Sandra Zoratti is Vice President, Marketing, Ricoh and manages a business created from former IBM and Ricoh companies located in Boulder, Colorado. Sandra built and launched the Precision Marketing practice from the ground up and is recognized as a thought leader in the area of Precision Marketing.

Currently, Sandra is driving Ricoh's co-branded initiatives with the Chief Marketing Officer Council to help senior marketers around the world optimize customer engage ment through the adoption of precision marketing practices. Sandra continues to lead the generation of in-market proof points to validate Precision Marketing practices with several companies which, as a result, produced double digit revenue increases and significant upticks in ROI.

Sandra gained global marketing experience at IBM in the highly successful design and launch of the 'Express' portfolio of offerings developed specifically for small and medium businesses (SMB). In this position, Sandra worked across all IBM brands and businesses charting IBM's formal entry into SMB markets. Her best practices approach has been adopted by several large corporations.

Prior to IBM, Sandra spent 15 years creating and executing marketing and business development initiatives worldwide for blue chip corporations including Avery Dennison and Westinghouse, as well as setting up her own private marketing practice. Sandra serves on several national and international boards and is a published author and frequent speaker.

Lee Gallagher is Director, Precision Marketing Solutions across Ricoh's multiple business lines. Lee's integrated marketing approach cuts through the cacophony of marketing messaging to deliver rock solid ROI. His efforts have placed him as a leader in strategy and design to some of the world's most highly respected brands.

Lee is frequently known to say, "The difficult is easy but it's the impossible that takes me three days" as he shares and leverages his past 18 years with IBM to influence his marketing efforts at Ricoh. At IBM, his unwavering commitment and passion led him to win every sales award available, including the coveted Lou Gerstner Award. In reviewing his career, Lee strongly believes the key to his success is and will continue to be, his drive to deliver relevant solutions and targeted, yet measured marketing to his customers.

Additionally, he blogs, conducts research and writes articles on how to deliver revenue through relevance by the implementation of The Precision Marketing Framework to deliver irrefutable ROI back to the business. Most recently his work has been discussed in the Wall Street Journal Radio, PBS, Business Week, and MSNBC. He has moved from Atlanta to Denver and is currently learning how to live at a higher elevation.

Introduction
Why Relevance is Relevant

There are many ways of going forward, but only one way of standing still.

FRANKLIN D ROOSEVELT

There's a backlash underway in today's economy. Consumers are in control. They are making it clear that they are tired of being deluged by a flood of irrelevant advertisements and marketing messages. Overwhelmed by ad fatigue and messaging mayhem, they are responding with digital video recorders to skip over unwanted commercials, using spam blockers to eliminate irrelevant e-mail and putting themselves on do-not-call lists to silence the endlessly ringing phone. They are even unsubscribing from e-mail lists that they once opted into as a connection to their companies of choice.

It's no wonder. Years ago, a 1978 study by Yankelovich found that the average American was confronted with more than 2,000 advertising messages per day. When the study was revisited in 2007, Yankelovich found that the number had soared to more than 5,000 messages per day.[1] Estimates from a study published in 2010 put the number at 16,000 advertisements per day.[2]

Here are a few more stats to consider:

- While 64% of consumers say promotional offers dominate both the e-mail and traditional mail they receive, only 41% view these as must-read communications.[3]
- Of the 91% of consumers who opt out or unsubscribe from e-mails, 46% are driven to brand defection because the messages are simply not relevant.[4]
- Forty-one per cent of consumers say they would consider ending a brand relationship owing to irrelevant promotions, and an additional 22% say they would definitely defect from the brand due to irrelevance.[5]

- Some 58% of vendors' marketing content is not relevant to potential buyers and reduces vendors' chances of closing a sale by 45%, according to a survey of IT buyers by the International Data Group.[6]

Consumers, apparently, have had enough and they are taking action. Power, as a result, is shifting. The customer is in control *and knows it*.

While product suppliers and mass marketers may have controlled the flow of communication in the past, consumers have started setting the terms under which conversations and interactions take place. Consumers are voting with their money and their attention. Every time they program the digital video recorder, opt out of an e-mail list or block a phone call, they are expressing their right to ignore the messages they find irrelevant. What's more, the influence of today's empowered consumers is spreading through social networks. By voicing opinions online with friends, family and the global internet community, consumers are – almost effortlessly and exponentially – influencing and defining the perception of a brand. Consumer conversations – not marketing messages – increasingly determine what gets attention and what gets ignored.

Confronting the power shift

Given these trends, companies run the risk of seeing returns on their marketing investments steadily dwindle. Marketers are already experiencing declining budgets and simultaneously facing an increasingly difficult set of market dynamics. According to Forrester Research, marketers list today's 'competitive, mature and unstable environment' as their top challenge.[7]

Perhaps it's not surprising that the tenures of chief marketing officers (CMOs) are so brief, averaging just 18 months, according to one study.[8] In a market that is becoming ever more hostile to their efforts, CMOs are struggling to drive growth and meet their numbers.

How do you engage consumers who are flat-out ignoring you? How do you confront today's buyer backlash? How do you attract new customers, strengthen relationships with existing ones and deliver an impressive return on your marketing investment? How, in other words, do you drive profitable growth in today's attention-starved economy?

The answers lie in one deceptively simple word: **relevance**.

The relevance requirement

Market research demonstrates that consumer attention and interest are directly proportional to the salience of the message. The more compelling, valuable and relevant you make your messages and offers, the more impactful the messages become – and the more likely it is that your prospective and existing customers will respond. As you present your brand in increasingly relevant ways, you drive increases in revenue, response and, ultimately, return on investment (ROI).

Relevance, in other words, is now a requirement for marketing success. Yet marketers continue to lag in acting upon the urgent need to align marketing and messaging to be relevant to their customers. When this is the case, marketers are putting their companies – and their jobs – in jeopardy. They are pursuing obsolete marketing approaches even as the outcomes associated with those approaches are clearly in decline.

Customers have growing power, leverage and influence. They have become adept at tuning out the irrelevant, and they are unwilling to listen to messages that don't matter to them.

That consumers are tuning out noise is obvious. Not only is this claim validated by research, but also it resonates with personal experience. People are more likely to pay attention to a message that speaks directly to their own personal concerns and desires than to a message that speaks blandly and broadly to a mass audience of which they happen to be part.

How to capitalize on this finding, however, is much less obvious.

The power of Precision Marketing

As we see it, marketers are now challenged to engage their customers on a new and relevant level. This is where the definition and concept of Precision Marketing gain momentum. Precision Marketing is a process that, if followed with the key building blocks described in this book, gives marketers the insights into customer behaviours that let them talk with customers in a relevant manner. The Precision Marketing framework relies heavily on several key factors, the first of which is the collection and analysis of data. Marketers are no longer in a position where they can randomly create interesting advertising campaigns; they must be aware of their customers and talk directly to them or risk driving them away. Marketers must create actionable customer insights to accomplish this objective. Collecting the customer data that give marketers the information they need to build strategies framed on customer insights is imperative to enable this objective. *Data enable actionable insights.* Consumers who are overwhelmed with irrelevant offers and messaging are less likely to deal with companies that don't know them.

Marketers cannot produce compelling messages in a vacuum. Rather, they must now employ customer insights to ensure that their communications are aligned with the preferences and priorities of their customers. Marketers must also learn to integrate their messages within an overall mix of channels – a mix that encompasses everything from direct mail to social media to mobile communication.

So why aren't more marketers implementing Precision Marketing today? On the basis of our work with numerous companies, we believe there are three key challenges to overcome:

1 The first challenge is collecting the correct data. Approximately 70% of marketers gather only demographic and location data,[9] which is not enough, because not all 40-year-old women in San Francisco are the same. Demographics and location by themselves are too imprecise. Today's critical insights must be drawn from such factors as customer preferences and behaviours; unfortunately these data points are obtained by a much lower percentage of marketers.

2 The second challenge is to act on the customer data that has been collected. Some marketers today may be collecting voluminous amounts of data, but they are often not aggregating and analysing that data to generate actionable insights. It is not enough for marketers to know what their customers prefer; marketers have to be able to predict their customers' needs and propensity to purchase.

3 The third challenge is execution and measuring results in order to test predictions. Here is where relevance plays a key role. Marketers must utilize highly relevant messaging and offers aligned to target customer segments. In addition, they must measure who converted, who did not, and, most importantly, why.

From our work with recognized firms in sectors such as banking, finance, telecommunications, insurance, publishing, hospitality and utilities, we have proved the power of Precision Marketing in real-world implementations across geographies, industries and applications. As advisers on marketing approaches to maximize customer engagement, we have learned how to meet these challenges and identify new growth opportunities. Our approach, which we call *Precision Marketing*, has produced extraordinary results for our clients in areas such as revenue, retention and ROI.

> Precision Marketing is about using data-driven insights to deliver the right message, to the right person, at the right time, via the right channel(s).

In this book we'll share our experiences, as well as research and evidence from others, on how to implement the principles of Precision Marketing.

Precision Marketing: why now?

There are multiple forces behind the emergence of Precision Marketing, but the most significant are economics, competition and technology.

Diminishing economic demand

One of the most troubling insights revealed by the recent financial collapse and ensuing recession was the degree to which consumer spending had been propped up by unsustainable debt. Between 2005 and 2007, personal savings rates fell to the lowest levels since the Great Depression.[10] However, consumers who had been emboldened by the seemingly endless rise in the value of their homes were soon laid low by the bursting of the real estate bubble. Rising unemployment rates further increased caution and restrained consumer spending. Naturally, consumers have been forced to save more of their earnings and spend their money much more carefully.

Plunging demand has forced companies to rethink how they acquire new customers and how they retain existing ones. Marketers have realized they won't be able to identify new customers without appealing to them in ways that address the individual's particular needs and interests. Marketers must, in other words, make their messages and offers relevant. They will not be able to continue meeting their growth targets without providing new dimensions of value to their customers. Marketers have also realized that retaining existing customers is, in most cases, more profitable than acquiring new customers. Businesses are now committed to ensuring that their most important customers remain loyal.

The techniques and strategies built into your Precision Marketing model will give your company the tools necessary to align your messaging with your goals.

Intensifying competition

Companies might be tempted to sit on their available cash and play it safe in a slow-growth economy. The problem with this strategy is that smart and savvy competitors will not be sitting still. Some companies will begin implementing new marketing approaches and business strategies that leverage customer data, triggering intense competition for consumers' attention and cash.

The most significant spending growth has been in the online marketing channels. As a result, companies are feverishly launching new marketing programmes using social media, viral approaches, personalized e-mail, paid search, behavioural targeting and other approaches to differentiate themselves from rivals.

No one wants to lose the edge in customer acquisition or surrender their existing customers to aggressive competitors. Online retail presents one example. In a study of shopper behaviour, Adobe found that shoppers 'need to feel like they are getting an "in-store" experience when they're "browsing" online'. Consequently, web-based retailers are competing by offering customized configurators and predictive shopping tools. 'High quality, large images, with zoom, spin, and color options emulate the "touch and feel" experience of shopping in-store, while the use of video can show products in real use, simulating a "knowledgeable" in-store clerk's live demonstrations.'[11]

Advancing technology

The onward march of technological progress is yet another factor in the growth of Precision Marketing, and it is playing out on many fronts.

One example that underscores this fact is the 2009 market forecast for business analytics and optimization, which puts the market size at $140 billion with a 7 per cent compound annual growth rate, which would produce an anticipated market size of $205 billion in 2015 (Figure 0.1).

On the basis of this forecast, big companies are placing big bets. IBM, Google, Microsoft, SAP and Oracle have invested multiple billions of dollars to acquire companies with data-based technological capabilities. In fact, IBM alone has invested $11 billion to acquire 18 data analytics-oriented companies since 2005. The worldwide market for business intelligence (BI) software was forecast to grow by 9.7 per cent to reach US $10.8 billion in 2011, according to Gartner's latest enterprise software forecast. Recognizing the undervalued nature of today's data assets, these leading companies are investing heavily and democratizing the tools of sophisticated analytics. As *The Economist* recently put it:

FIGURE 0.1

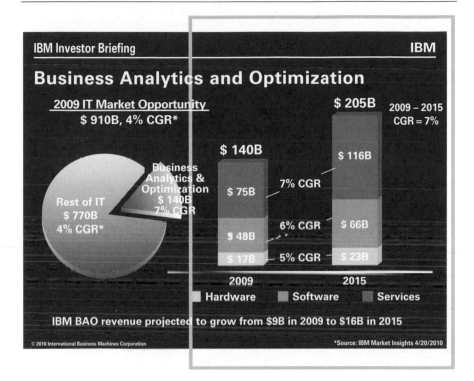

A few years ago such technologies, called 'business intelligence', were available only to the world's biggest companies. But as the price of computing and storage has fallen and software systems have got better and cheaper, the technology has moved into the mainstream. Companies are collecting more data than ever before. In the past they were kept in different systems that were unable to talk to each other, such as finance, human resources or customer management. Now the systems are being linked, and companies are using data-mining techniques to get a complete picture of their operations – a 'single version of the truth', as the industry likes to call it. That allows firms to operate more efficiently, pick out trends and improve their forecasting.[12]

Such technological advances are enabling companies to leverage their previously undervalued data to create actionable, predictive customer insights. Data aggregating, analysing and modelling tools are required to produce these customer insights, which form the technological foundation of Precision Marketing.

Although some marketers believe that the ability to leverage data analytics is only in the domain of powerful IT companies, that is not so. Data analytics technology is no longer in the sole domain of the IT department. Smart marketers are incorporating an array of analytical technologies across all of their marketing practices to drive relevant, engaging content and predictive customer profiles. Marketers who embrace data, analytics and campaign measurement will be well positioned to provide higher returns back to the business.

By addressing and overcoming these challenges, Precision Marketing is possible. Marketers can employ data-driven marketing techniques, although it is a journey that takes time. The journey may require some marketing practices to be changed, but it does not require an extravagant budget. The approach we present in this book will enable you to achieve far more with and from your existing resources. By moving in the data-driven direction, you'll be taking steps that will engage your customers and enhance your marketing results. This is the future – and the future is now.

Tesco's triumph

One company that has embraced Precision Marketing techniques and, as a result, has achieved spectacular results, is London-based retailer Tesco. Throughout the book, we will be examining the experiences of companies in a variety of industries and sharing their stories – both successes and failures – to illustrate our concepts and help you in understanding and implementing the ideas. Let's begin with a look at the experiences and practices of Tesco.

In its early days, Tesco was known as a low-price grocery store. 'Pile it high and sell it cheap' was the chain's motto. But Tesco executives realized that a low-cost strategy by itself was not sustainable. In the early 1990s, Tesco was losing customers to competitors. Why? Tesco realized it didn't know who its customers were. Before 1995, Tesco did not know whether its customers were young or old, rich or poor, how much they bought from Tesco, how much they bought from competitors, or whether the latest promotion or price cut was helping or hurting the bottom line.

To remedy this situation, Terry Leahy, then a marketing executive at Tesco, launched the Clubcard, a loyalty card programme. Clubcard gives customers rebates, coupons and discounts in exchange for customers providing information about themselves and using the card every time they shop. Customers share their personal shopping interests and preferences, particularly when they use their cards to make trackable purchases in any of Tesco's stores.[13]

Tesco has since proved to be a master at leveraging these insights. With more than 16 million cards in use in Britain, Tesco can closely watch what its shoppers are purchasing. Tesco executives then explore linkages between the products people currently buy and the ones they might be persuaded to buy next. As *The Economist* explains, Tesco can

> lavish attention on customers by giving them discounts on things that they buy routinely. Each cardholder gets a letter at the end of each quarter containing vouchers worth roughly 1% of what they have spent. But they also get coupons that entitle them to discounts on products that Tesco's database, working much like the software that powers Amazon.com, suggests they might like.[14]

Competitors dismissed Clubcard as an unsustainable discount programme that would sap Tesco's profits. What detractors failed to realize was that Tesco was buying and compiling data that enabled it to understand its customers and create much more relevant messages and offerings.

In the years since its introduction, Tesco has used Clubcard data to:

- achieve coupon redemption rates of 20–40% compared to the average 2%;
- expand into non-food categories;
- create new brands;
- become the largest online grocer in the United Kingdom;
- grow from less than 600 stores to more than 4,000 stores in 13 countries.[15]

Today, half of all British households have a Clubcard, and Tesco has grown to be the third-largest retailer in the world. And how did marketing executive Terry Leahy fare? He became Chief Executive Officer of Tesco and was knighted.

Three eras of modern marketing

How has marketing evolved to transition into Precision Marketing? For this, let's take a brief look at the history of marketing and its transformation during the recent past. Over the past 40 years of marketing history, three major eras emerged: the Creative Era, the Direct Era and the Relevance Era.

The first – the Creative Era – arose in the 1960s and 1970s with the insights of such luminaries as Bill Bernbach. One of the three founders of Doyle Dane Bernbach (DDB), he directed ad campaigns such as 'Think Small' for

Volkswagen's Beetle and 'We Try Harder' for Avis. He also introduced consumers to 'Mikey,' a little boy who loved the breakfast cereal Life. Bernbach is legendary for having challenged the research-driven premises of conventional advertising. 'Logic and over-analysis can immobilize and sterilize an idea,' he said. 'It's like love – the more you analyze it, the faster it disappears.'[16]

The second – the Direct Era – was driven by modern information technology such as database software and even desktop computing. Arising in the early 1980s, it revolved around direct marketing and various direct response techniques. Data-driven approaches – tied up in recency, frequency and monetary (RFM) scores of customer behaviour and opportunity – influenced a whole new generation of marketers. In one speech, Les Wunderman, arguably the father of direct marketing, pointed out that the computer 'can know and remember as much marketing detail about 200,000,000 consumers as did the owner of a crossroads general store about his handful of customers.'[17] These innovators would later leverage the power of internet marketing.

Flash forward to the present. The consumer is in revolt. The consumer, as we've said, is now overwhelmed and feels mistreated and disrespected. Consumers, in fact, are more demanding than ever. They have a multiplicity of choices but a diminishing amount of trust and confidence. This simple fact sets the stage for a new era in marketing: the Relevance Era.

The Relevance Era

Today's important era of transformational change will revolve around the customer, respecting the needs, preferences and priorities of the individual. Relevance will close the chasm between creative and direct marketing, leveraging customer insight to produce truly valuable content and communication that engage the buyer through highly relevant customer touchpoints.

Smart marketers at companies such as Tesco, Caesar's Entertainment Corporation (formerly branded Harrah's), ING Bank, 1-800-Flowers and Amazon.com are putting the customer at the centre of their marketing activities with the knowledge and realization that it's *always* about the customer. Following the principles described in this book will enable you to join this powerful movement, developing the perspectives, skills and capabilities necessary to deliver more powerful marketing results.

The first chapter, 'Getting Relevant', explains the irrefutable role of relevance as a powerful enabler in transforming your customer relationships and business results. It also explains the dangerous risks of continued irrelevance. In this chapter we will show why companies must rethink their customer approach and adopt Precision Marketing.

Chapter 2, 'The Precision Marketing Journey,' lays out the six steps of our Precision Marketing Framework. This framework provides a practical guide to adopting an analytical approach to your business and marketing practices.

Chapter 3, 'Step One: Determine Your Objective,' walks you through the first step of the Precision Marketing journey. This step represents the foundation for any Precision Marketing implementation, and we will help you establish objective-setting practices.

Chapter 4, 'Step Two: Gather Data,' describes how organizations can collect data, both internally and externally, and set the stage for turning these data into valuable, actionable customer insights.

Chapter 5, 'Step Three: Analyse and Model,' guides you through the process of developing and utilizing analytical models and algorithms to truly leverage data to enhance your customer engagement and drive marketing and business results.

Chapter 6, 'Step Four: Strategize,' outlines ways to utilize the output from your data analytics to develop your strategy around specific customer targets, precise content development, relevant messaging, campaign design and supporting tactics.

Chapter 7, 'Step Five: Deploy,' focuses on the implementation of your Precision Marketing campaign. We'll show how the field of marketing is rapidly changing and how many of the greatest career opportunities are opening up for people who can turn customer insight into customer engagement.

Chapter 8, 'Step Six: Measure,' will focus on gathering and learning from the metrics of your Precision Marketing campaign in order to factually and objectively understand what worked and what did not work. Measuring is about how to learn and how to improve through experience.

Chapter 9, 'A Precision Marketing case study,' walks you through the full-scale Tesco implementation of the Precision Marketing journey, step by step. This case study will showcase the business benefits possible for companies that are willing to make the journey.

Chapter 10, 'The Precision Marketer's Moment,' is about your personal contributions and growth as a Precision Marketer. We'll show how the field of marketing is rapidly changing and how many of the greatest opportunities for making an impact and progressing are realized by people who can turn data into customer insight, then into relevance, into customer engagement and finally into revenue and ROI.

The conclusion is our call to action for you, our reader. We hope that this book will inspire you and motivate you to take your first steps towards Precision Marketing so that the journey – and the rewards that it offers you and your business – can be fully realized.

In this book, you will see how today's leading performers are beginning to recognize, identify and capitalize on many of the concepts of Precision Marketing to set themselves apart and reach the next level of growth. You will also learn what must happen and what steps must be taken to unify the now disparate worlds of creative and direct marketing. And you'll discover how all of these insights can be applied in your own particular situation – helping both your company and your career.

Notes

1 Louise Story, Anywhere the Eye Can See, It's Likely to See an Ad, *New York Times*, 15 January 2007.

2 Emily Osburne, Be Unforgettable!, *Toastmaster*, March 2010, p. 20.

3 CMO Council, *Why Relevance Drives Response and Relationships: Using the power of Precision Marketing to better engage customers*, 2009.

4 Ibid.

5 Ibid.

6 Michael Cannon, Nine Silver Bullets to Increase Marketing's Relevance, Silver Bullet Group, Walnut Creek, CA, 2010.

7 Jaap Favier, The Challenges of CMOs in 2008, Forrester Research, 28 March 2008.

8 Spencer Stuart, CMO Tenure: Slowing down the revolving door, 2004 [Online] **http://content.spencerstuart.com/sswebsite/pdf/lib/CMO_brochureU1.pdf**.

9 CMO Council, The Leaders in Loyalty: Feeling the love from the loyalty clubs, 2009.

10 Lloyd de Vries, Savings at Lowest Rate Since Depression, CBSNews.com, February 2007.

11 Adobe Scene 7 Viewer Study: What shoppers want, January 2010.

12 *The Economist*, A Special Report on Managing Information, February 2010.

13 Jackie Fenn and Mark Raskino, *Mastering the Hype Cycle: How to choose the right innovation at the right time*, Gartner Inc., Harvard Business Press, Boston, MA, 2008.

14 *The Economist*, This Sceptered Aisle, 4 August 2005.

15 Rick Ferguson, Lost in the Supermarket, *Colloquy*, Summer 2006.

16 Wikipedia entry: William Bernbach [Online]
http://en.wikipedia.org/wiki/William_Bernbach.

17 Wunderman.com, Substance: Quotations from our founder, 2010
[Online] **http://www.themarketingsite.com/content/
10034_substance_quotations_from_our_founder.pdf**.

Getting Relevant

Continuous improvement is better than delayed perfection.
MARK TWAIN

In this chapter, you will learn:

- the definition of Precision Marketing;

- how Amazon is using the principles of Precision Marketing and is positioning itself to increase revenues per customer;

- the risks and repercussions companies face when using poorly targeted promotions;

- what a relevant message is and how three companies in different industries created relevant, precisely targeted messages.

In the overwhelming din of messaging mayhem today, attention is a scarce resource. Consumers are in control and they vote with their dollars, their voice and their attention. They are selecting companies with which they will communicate and transact on the basis of the relevance of those companies' communications. We see innovators in the marketplace who are practising Precision Marketing by using relevance as the catalyst to cut through the cacophony in order to reach and fully engage customers. Companies, as demonstrated in the following example with Amazon, use relevance to retain current customers, maximize the revenue potential per customer, help to acquire new customers and build long-term customer loyalty. Amazon is an innovator in the application of Precision Marketing and is a highly appropriate place to start our discussion of how companies get relevant.

Amazon knows how to get relevant

Amazon knows what you're thinking. Amazon can see what you searched for, what you are looking at, what you wish you could get, what you bought, and what you didn't buy. Amazon's Wish List system lets prospects and customers enter products that they would like to buy (or to have loved ones buy for them for birthdays or holidays). The searching, browsing and Wish List data give Amazon powerful insight into purchase intentions. Amazon can then create relevant and highly targeted e-mails to customers to alert them about price changes for items on their Wish List or to provide information on new products or on products related to those the customer wants.

Capitalizing on its insights, Amazon now reigns supreme among online book retailers and over the years has branched out into many other forms of online merchandise. What is particularly impressive is how the company has managed to hold prices in line with those of Wal-Mart – on everything from the latest best-seller to the holiday toy that is in greatest demand – while offering its customers a more personal and convenient shopping experience.

As a result, Amazon's growth has consistently topped 30 per cent annually. What's more, Amazon is positioned to grow even more as consumers shift to making more purchases online. In the retail sales arena, total online retail sales currently represent only 6 per cent of annual retail spending.[1] It seems clear, however, that consumer spending will increasingly shift to online purchases as more individuals obtain broadband internet services and become comfortable with online shopping. Amazon's strengths as a provider of relevant offers could prove to be crucial as the battle for market share and share of wallet continues to escalate in the coming years.[2]

Much of what we see at Amazon mimics the concepts and strategies of Precision Marketing. Amazon does now what every company must begin to do. As Amazon's success impressively suggests, to survive you must *get relevant*.

What will *you* do to build profitable and enduring relationships with your customers? How can *you* build trust and credibility with your prospects? What must *you* do to produce successful and sustainable marketing results and spur growth?

As a marketer, you must learn how to capture and mine data about your customers and prospects. Then you must leverage these insights to produce messages, offers and value that reflect the preferences and priorities of those you wish to engage. That's what Amazon did. That's what Amazon does.

Unfortunately, many marketing and customer-oriented groups in businesses today have taken only rudimentary steps in this direction. Marketers don't know their customers in any great depth, nor do they interact with them in a truly relevant fashion. Many businesses are prone to producing bland and unfocused marketing messages that are far from compelling, provocative or persuasive. Businesses spend a great deal of money to reach the wrong person at the wrong time with the wrong message or offer. Why is this happening?

The 1 per cent solution

One core challenge is the way that many marketers evaluate their results. They tend to judge the efficacy of a marketing campaign on three simple variables: the channel cost, the response rate and the incremental income from a positive response. If the piece rate is inexpensive enough and the income from a response is lavish enough (as it is for credit cards, cell phones, computer software and a host of other high-dollar goods), then some marketers think they don't have to care about relevance. What is the harm if the message is irrelevant to 99 per cent of the recipients, they reason, as long as the 1 per cent who do respond make the campaign a 'success'? That's the question an enormous number of marketers must begin asking themselves, because the damage inflicted by irrelevant messages is indeed severe. The rise of ultra-low-cost marketing channels such as e-mail and social networks opened the floodgates for ineffective and irrelevant communications. The internet made it so inexpensive to reach millions of potential customers that many marketers began to think they could inundate peoples' inboxes without consequence. As a result, if even a minuscule percentage of the messages led to a response, the campaign showed a profit.

While marketers applaud the 1 per cent of consumers who do respond, they ignore – at their peril – the behaviour of the 99 per cent who do not. The intrusive nature of irrelevant messaging leads the 99 per cent who do not respond not only to ignore the messages but to take steps that become detrimental to the company. Customers block phone calls, block e-mail and

FIGURE 1.1   Choose your target: 1% or 99%

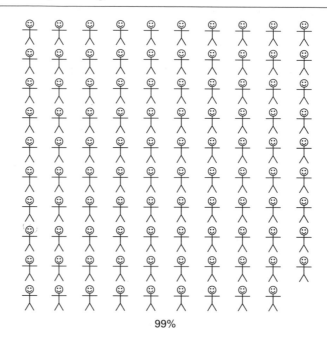

1%   99%

cease to be loyal to companies that speak generically to them. Irrelevant marketing carries a serious, if somewhat hidden, cost.

Data on customer loyalty confirm the damage caused by irrelevance. Here is a chilling thought for marketers: for the average brand, more than half of all loyal consumers in 2007 did not remain loyal in 2008. According to the study 'Losing loyalty: the consumer defection dilemma' conducted by Catalina Marketing's Pointer Media Network in conjunction with the CMO Council, approximately one-third of all highly loyal consumers in 2007 completely defected to another brand in the same consumer packaged goods category in 2008. 'The wishful thought that "my loyals will stay my loyals" – that highly loyal consumers, by and large, remain loyal from year to year – is no longer a comfortable assumption,' the study noted. 'The truth is that consumer churn and defection are consistent problems in today's consumer packaged goods marketplace.'[3]

Companies pay a steep price for high levels of brand defection, particularly in recessionary times. If the major brands tracked in the 'Losing loyalty' study had retained their highly loyal customers from 2007, their 2008 observable revenues would have increased from 5 per cent to 25 per cent, according to the study's authors. That is a great deal of growth to sacrifice, particularly in a difficult economy when *any* growth is hard to realize.[4]

What if customers controlled your marketing?

What if your customers were in control of your marketing budget? That may sound crazy, but posing such a question opens a new perspective for you. The fact is, customers are more and more in control of both their spending and their media consumption habits. Companies that respect customer power and provide customers with what they actually want will outperform and potentially outlive companies that assault them with irrelevant messages. It is much wiser to use your strategy to make customers the centre of your marketing efforts.

> Do your messages predict and anticipate your customers' needs or next actions? Are the marketing messages consistent with the goods and services the customer actually wants, chooses, and receives?

What is a relevant message?

Looking through the eyes of your customer will provide you with the lens necessary to achieve relevance. When you hit the relevance target, your revenues will grow, customer loyalty will surge, and you will achieve significant improvement in your business results. If you miss the target, you will be forced to explain to your board why precious assets were spent without a return back to the company.

Within the deafening barrage of messaging today, some companies do create communication that gets heard, gets seen and changes behaviour. *Relevance* is the key differentiator that separates successful marketing from wasteful marketing. Relevant messages resonate with the customer, speak to their unmet needs and reach the person in the right way, at the right time and with the right meaningful information, no matter what the medium.

When marketers link relevant messaging to customers who are ready to buy, their actions generate revenue.

Relevance is in the eye of the customer. When the customer sees a message that provides meaning and value to him or her, then – and only then – is the message relevant. Marketers can't declare that a message is relevant by putting 'URGENT & CONFIDENTIAL' in the subject line or on the envelope. Instead, they must make the message have true value to the customer. The fact that relevance is personal to the customer means that marketers must make their messages personal to the customer. Precision Marketing provides a four-level continuum of precision strategies (explained in detail in Chapter 5) that companies have used and can use to increase relevance. Old-style personalization – just slapping the person's name in the messages – does not create relevance.

In this new era the rules of customer engagement and communication have changed dramatically. Messaging can now be effective only if customers see it as personally relevant. This need for relevance is imperative regardless of which communication channel marketers use. As a recent study by the CMO Council found, 'Today's consumer wants timely and contextual messages, and clearly values opt-in, personal communications.'[5]

In response to the study's survey questions, consumers overwhelmingly stated that, regardless of the marketing channel, relevance and individualization were valued, if not required, to build an enduring relationship.

What are the risks of irrelevancy?

Almost all consumers (91 per cent) report that they opt out or unsubscribe to e-mails at some point. What's worse, they are no longer just tuning out irrelevant messages. Instead, consumers are actively demonstrating that they are overwhelmed by all the messaging. They are voting with their purses and potentially defecting from brands. According to the CMO Council, 63 per cent of consumers stated that they would consider ending a brand relationship because of irrelevance.[6] *Each irrelevant message creates a higher relevance hurdle for all subsequent messages.*

Consider the following different ways that customers can respond when a company has been sending them irrelevant messages and offers.

Customer response 1: blocking

First, a 2009 CMO study revealed that 73 per cent of consumers still receive promotions for products they have already purchased.[7] By any measure,

73 per cent is a staggering statistic. If your messages are irrelevant, then the chances are that they are in the 'don't read, don't bother' category in consumers' busy lives. Moreover, if a consumer realizes they've put your company in the 'don't read, don't bother' category and your company continues to clutter their inbox, then the customer may unsubscribe or block your company's e-mail messages, defect from your brand or, worse, voice their complaints on their blogs and to the internet community.

Marketers also make the mistake of assuming that if their customers haven't opted out, the marketing messages being sent are effective. This is a dangerous assumption, however, because many subscribers are at the 'unsubscribe threshold,' and that extra e-mail or two is the straw that breaks subscription's back and leads them to unsubscribe.

Customer response 2: taking revenge

Even when blocking messages, nearly one-third of consumers stated that they don't trust the 'unsubscribe' links in e-mail messages.[8] In other cases, companies make the unsubscribe process so unpleasant that consumers don't use it. So instead of unsubscribing to unwanted e-mail, 26 per cent of consumers click the 'report spam' button, according to a 2008 JupiterResearch study.[9] In this sense, consumers are actually striking back at companies that send them too much e-mail or irrelevant e-mail by logging spam complaints against them. These complaints impact the company's ability to reach other customers because collaborative spam filtering and blacklisting block the company's messages from reaching other customers' inboxes as well.

Customer response 3: raising legal barriers to communication

Excessive and intrusive marketing has led consumers to ask for governmental actions to regulate or curtail marketing activities. For example, in response to the rising volume of complaints about intrusive telemarketing calls, the US Federal Trade Commission created a National Do Not Call Registry in 2003.[10] Consumers eagerly registered some 191 million US telephone numbers. In other cases, legislation impedes the actions of marketers; the United States' CANSPAM Act of 2003 and the United Kingdom's Data Protection Act 1998 are examples of this kind of legislation.[11] Each new piece of legislation, executive action or unfavourable judicial ruling raises the costs of all marketing communications for everyone and restricts the opportunities for relevant marketing practices.

Customer response 4: losing loyalty and defecting from the brand

The most serious impact of irrelevant messaging is loss of loyalty. While your mass messaging may be earning money on the 1 per cent of customers who do respond, that irrelevant messaging may be losing you money on the 99 per cent who are disgruntled non-responders. The loyalty results are even worse for those who take the step of unsubscribing. Among the people who unsubscribe, nearly half defect from the brand as a result of irrelevant messages, according to the CMO Council's poll of consumers.[12]

Companies that 'get it'

Customers want to do business with companies that understand them and their needs. As Forrester data revealed, the top two reasons for opening an e-mail were needs and interests.[13] Everyone knows and appreciates the difference between an insider who understands, who was there, who 'gets it' and an outsider who doesn't understand, who hasn't lived it, or who is clueless.

'Customers expect you to apply the information you know about them and to continue to learn from the relationship,' note Tom Hannigan and Christina Palendrano, customer relationship management specialists writing in *Information Management* magazine.[14] That means using demographic, historical and predictive data to create relevant, engaging messages. 'They don't want their time wasted with irrelevant or inappropriate offers, and neither do you.' That's all well and good, but what does it mean? Creating relevant marketing means understanding the customer and what is most important to them. Here are three examples from three different industries to show you how companies achieve relevance.

Breckenridge creates a home away from home

The Breckenridge Lodging Association, a network of hotels, resorts and lodges, customizes its communications on the basis of a customer's previous purchasing habits. For example, the Breckenridge Lodging Association carefully tracks and records the hotel and lodging establishments in which a customer has stayed. It then sends the customer information on those resorts and other similar ones. When the customer calls to make a reservation, the Breckenridge Lodging Association automatically checks to see whether the customer's favourite resort is available. If the customer's first choice of lodging is not available, then the Association quickly suggests the next closest match. Although the hotels are all competitors, the Association gives the customer the impression that no one is trying to push them towards one property or another or sell them something they don't want.

By tracking past purchases, the Association creates relevant marketing that is consistent with the *customer*'s wants, not the hoteliers' wants. Because almost 65 per cent of Breckenridge's visitors are repeat guests, the hotels and the association know that high-quality, relevant personal service creates loyalty to the ski area, which is a long-term winning strategy.[15] The lesson from the Breckenridge Lodging Association case is for Precision Marketers to be customer-centric and use the customer's purchase history to generate future relevant offers.

Smooth Fitness gets to know its customers

Smooth Fitness is an online retailer that sells high-ticket exercise equipment such as treadmills and elliptical machines. The company set as its Precision Marketing objective *to attract new customers*.

The company's first challenge was to identify the visitors to its website. Smooth Fitness's web traffic tends to come from many different segments and subsets. However, the company had no way of identifying the segments to which individual website visitors belonged, and so it presented the same promotional messaging to all visitors. The company realized that it could enhance conversion rates and increase the return on investment if it could identify individual visitors and present them with relevant messages and offers that better reflected each visitor's particular interests.

With this goal in mind, Smooth Fitness utilized behavioural targeting technology capable of automatically matching relevant content with individual visitors. By providing content that featured flagship products, lifestyle imagery and call-to-action elements, the company's behavioural targeting solution determined which messages to serve to which customer segments. Smooth Fitness's technology dynamically leverages user data such as IP address, day and time of visit, referral information, and real-time website activity to show the most targeted and relevant content to each visitor.

Initial results started to emerge just one month after Smooth Fitness began using this approach. The company achieved a 12 per cent click-through rate increase relative to the random distribution of content. In the second month of deployment, the company produced a 48 per cent lift. By the third month the lift had reached 123 per cent. Meanwhile, conversions were up 8 per cent, revenues per visit were up 12 per cent and average order values were up nearly 20 per cent (Figure 1.2). Given the seasonality of Smooth Fitness's business, this approach has enabled the company to increase sales in the lean summer months as it strengthened its planning for winter months when sales tend to be significantly stronger.[16]

Behavioural targeting also enabled the marketing team to play a more strategic and valued role in the company. 'Having the ability to target our traffic sources automatically, and allowing the behavioural targeting engine to run continuously, generates a powerful ROI for us,' says Keith Menear, VP of Internet Sales and Marketing at Smooth Fitness. 'It frees up my team's resources to focus on other activities, while still delivering measurable and impactful conversion results.'[17]

The key lesson from the Smooth Fitness case is that behavioural targeting lets you deliver the right message to each customer and increase customer engagement.

Royal Canin Canada leads the pack with relevant information

Marketing messages that add to a customer's understanding of a brand help build customer confidence in the company. Marketers who give that power to customers see that power returned.

Royal Canin Canada is a company that makes several dozen varieties of dog and cat food that are specially tailored to meet the needs of different pets. The company has invested millions in research on animal nutrition to create foods designed for the unique nutritional needs of different breeds, different sizes, different ages and specific medical needs. The company even has several formulations for breeders and veterinary kennels.

Despite the variety of specialized offerings, Royal Canin needed to differentiate itself from the competitive pack of hundreds of pet food makers and the cacophony of pet food marketing. Royal Canin knows that any pet food maker can place a generic picture of a German shepherd on the outside of the bag. 'We have German shepherd food, [and if it has a] German shepherd picture on it, people think it's a marketing ploy,' says Andrew Cannon, a direct marketing associate. Royal Canin uses its knowledge of the optimal nutritional ingredients to tailor its natural pet food to the exact nutritional

FIGURE 1.2 Smooth Fitness relevance results

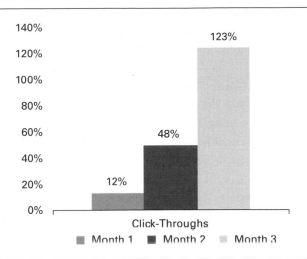

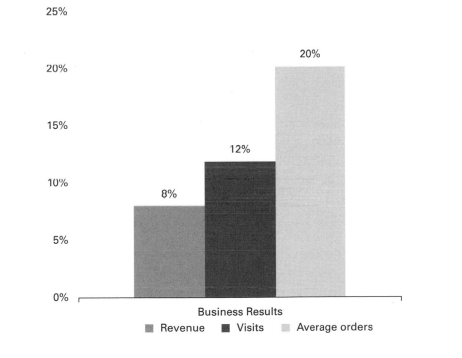

needs of each breed. The marketing challenge is to demonstrate Royal Canin's unique nutritional expertise and knowledge to pet owners.

So, to engage with buyers of its premium pet food, Royal Canin created the 'PetFirst!' e-mail programme. The company introduces the existence of the e-mail programme at pet food retailers and on bags of its food. The pet owner enters the names, dates of birth, weights and breeds of each of their dogs or cats when they join the programme. The company then sends e-mails that are customized to both the person and their pets.

Royal Canin knows that customers dislike marketing mayhem, so the company explicitly lists what will be arriving – and when – in the inbox when the customer signs up for PetFirst! membership. Typical e-mail frequency is twice a month. From the start of the relationship, Royal Canin begins to build trust with its subscribers. Royal Canin clearly knows that it needs to look at its marketing messages from the customer's perspective. Cannon says:

> Simply talking about product benefits isn't good enough. Our constant challenge is to be more relevant to pet owners, to help them better understand the needs of their pets, what makes their dog or cat different, before we start talking about how we can help. It's like consultative selling – we put needs first and become a trusted adviser to pet owners.[18]

This means focusing on the needs of the customer and their pet rather than the desire of the company to sell more pet food.

Royal Canin provides relevant content in several ways. The e-mail messages speak to both the owner and the pet by name. More importantly, Royal Canin provides content specific to the pet's age and breed based on the company's deep knowledge of the customer. For example, when a puppy is 10 months old the company sends a new 'Life Stage Guide' introducing information about the changing nutritional needs of the pet. Yorkshire terrier owners, for instance, learn that their dogs have powerful teeth deeply set in a rather small jaw, making the breed relatively susceptible to gum disease. The educated details are what make the difference, and Royal Canin conveys valuable, specific information tailored to the needs of each pet owner.

In particular, Royal Canin uses veterinary research to create more informative and thus more relevant Precision Marketing messages. Royal Canin uses a myriad of data – such as bone structure, activity level, longevity, jaw structure and specific diseases that afflict specific breeds – when it crafts individualized content for each pet and pet owner. Royal Canin uses data on the pet's breed and then ties those data to medical facts about specific product characteristics (shape, size, protein content, nutrient balance, etc) of each type of pet food it sells. For example, the food for Labrador retrievers is designed to take longer to chew, which helps reduce that breed's tendency towards overeating and obesity.[19] Finally, the company also sends e-mails celebrating each pet's birthday to add an emotional connection, not just an informational one.

By delivering relevant information, Royal Canin created a 95 per cent open rate and an 80 per cent click-through rate (Figure 1.3). 'With the core group of subscribers we've attracted over the past few months, it's been extremely successful,' says Cannon.[20]

FIGURE 1.3 Royal Canin results from relevance

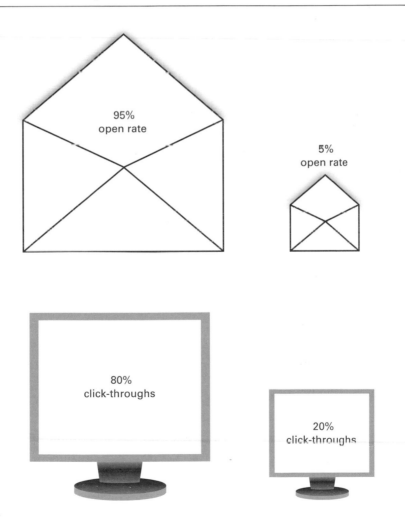

The key message to take from the Royal Canin case is: if you want people to read your messages, you need to give them something worth reading, tied precisely to their needs based on your knowledge of them.

Making it powerful, making it precise

These examples emonstrate the power of what we call Precision Marketing. *Precision Marketing is defined as using data-driven insights to deliver the right message to the right person at the right time in the right channel(s).* Precision Marketing is an approach that emphasizes the power of the personal and the results of the relevant. With Precision Marketing, marketers customize their communications, interactions and offerings to reflect what their buyers have told them about themselves and what the marketers can ascertain about them from the insights they have generated. In other words, Precision Marketers get relevant.

As economies mature and competition intensifies, the pressure to appeal to the individual needs, preferences and priorities of prospects and customers has never been greater. Indeed, customers often expect this now – and their expectations are perpetually rising.

We are coming full circle. One hundred years ago, the owner of the corner store knew your name, knew your preferences and made personal recommendations. He or she might even have given you store credit or filled your bag for you. Then we entered an era of mass communication and mass production. Industrialized factories pumped out consumer goods that met our generally shared desire for greater comfort and convenience. Madison Avenue advertisers relied on mass media – broadcast networks, national magazines and large-circulation dailies – to reach us with messages that had mass appeal.

Now we seem to be returning to an economic environment in which buyers expect to receive personal treatment from their product and service providers. Relationships matter again and can become even more successful when they are relationships built on rich databases and mediated with advanced communications technology.

To succeed now, marketers must get personal and relevant. According to the CMO Council,

> messaging to the mass market in general is simply not going to cut through the clutter and deluge of direct mail, advertising, Internet, email and cold calling overtures. Customers are looking for a sign that the companies soliciting them

FIGURE 1.4 Deriving Relevance from Customer Insights

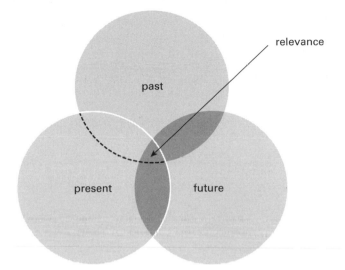

know something about them, and actually care about and understand their personal circumstances and dynamics, and, savvy customers today are very good at tuning out commercial noise and being more selective with whom they do business.[21]

As we have said, Precision Marketing is about reaching customers with the right message or offer in the right channel at the right time. Precision Marketing is also about integrating the customer insights, including all previous interactions, so that present and future interactions are deeply relevant (Figure 1.4).

If marketers are to excel in the Relevance Era, they will need to dramatically re-engineer their marketing approaches. First, marketers still have to acknowledge the fact that it's easier than ever for customers to defect and that revenue growth will be ever more difficult to obtain. Smart marketers, in fact, list today's 'competitive, mature and unstable environment' as their top market challenge.[22]

Next, marketers must come to grips with the growing demands and expectations of their prospects and customers. As consumers experience increasingly relevant interaction in hospitality, banking, telecommunications, insurance and other sectors, they will begin to expect such treatment across the board and will tolerate nothing less. Product and service providers will be under increasing pressure to provide compelling and customized experiences to remain competitive.[23]

Finally, marketers need to embrace the new strategies, methods and technologies that are transforming today's customer relationships. These new capabilities will not only enable marketers to engage their customers with greater relevance but also enable them to track and measure performance with greater precision. Just as customer expectations will rise, so too will expectations in the boardroom and the executive suite. Marketing performance, in this Relevance Era, must rise to new and impressive levels.

Achieving relevance through Precision Marketing

One of the most consistent factors in all of the successful efforts discussed in this book is the commitment of organizations to gain greater precision in their marketing and customer engagement efforts. Precision Marketing, as we see it, is an approach that revolves around leveraging buyer insights to produce relevant messages, offers and solutions.

Precision Marketing is a significant step beyond conventional marketing in that it blends data technology with the creative process as it concentrates on engaging customers in an increasingly targeted – often individualized – fashion.

Precision Marketing is also a significant step beyond individualized, one-to-one marketing. For example, in their 1993 book *The One to One Future*, Don Peppers and Martha Rogers presciently envisioned and articulated this one-to-one trend. They carried forward the proposition that customer relationships were far more valuable than anyone realized, and that marketers must begin to engage their customers in a truly personal fashion. 'To work successfully in a one-to-one world, you will have to calculate your success one customer at a time,' they wrote, thus inspiring a generation of marketers.[24]

Often erroneously confused with one-to-one marketing, Precision Marketing is a scientific approach using data-driven, behavioural-based predictive techniques. One-to-one marketing and Precision Marketing are different in that Precision Marketing goes beyond the capabilities of one-to-one marketing. Precision Marketing continually finds distinct customer behaviours that have been overlooked by traditional marketing techniques and drives incremental revenue and return back to the business. In contrast, one-to-one marketing moved messaging from generic to personalized – for example, from 'Dear Resident' to 'Dear Amanda' – in the hope of building a deeper relationship. Precision Marketing uses a six-step process that includes advanced scientific methods and comprehensive analysis. The process will, first, help marketers predict Amanda's propensity to respond; second, it will help marketers understand when she will most likely respond; third, it will predict which offers she will most likely purchase; and finally, it will help marketers build predictive insights about Amanda's future buying behaviour.

Most importantly, Precision Marketing is the way to produce stronger results. More than 56 per cent of marketers believe that relevant communications outperform traditional mass market approaches, according to research from the CMO Council. Marketers in technology and internet-related fields rated their customized initiatives even higher, with 63 per cent stating that customization had outperformed mass-market delivery (Figure 1.5).[25]

The drive to bring new levels of relevance to marketing is clearly elevated by today's harsh economic climate and the thin margin of error now facing all companies. All marketers are being challenged to keep and grow their existing customers. Marketers won't be able to meet that objective unless they engage their customers in deeply relevant ways. Such demands will inevitably encourage marketers to invest in Precision Marketing initiatives, which will be discussed in greater depth in the next chapter.

FIGURE 1.5

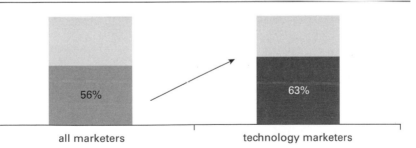

56%	63%
all marketers	technology marketers

Key takeaway messages from Chapter 1, 'Getting relevant'

- In the overwhelming noise that is our current world, the scarcest resource is attention.

- Companies can cut through the clutter by using highly relevant content and communications based on customer insights.

- The risks of irrelevancy are enormous, as 91 per cent of consumers are opting out of e-mails and an astounding 63 per cent are liable to disengage from brands because of irrelevant messaging. These trends, at the very least, are a stark wake-up call for marketers.

- Consumers vote with their purses, voices and attention and are proactively taking steps to tune out messaging with actions such as:
  - blocking;
  - taking revenge;
  - raising legal barriers to communication;
  - losing loyalty and defecting from the brand.

- Customers want to do business with companies that understand them and their needs. Companies can use the customer's purchase history to generate future relevant offers, and they can create messages that customers will read by focusing on what customers want to know – not just on what the company wants them to know.

- Precision Marketing means:
  - using data-driven insights to deliver the right message to the right person at the right time in the right channel(s);
  - leveraging customer insights, including all previous interactions, so that present and future interactions are deeply relevant;
  - blending data technology with the creative process to engage customers in an increasingly targeted – often individualized – fashion.

Notes

1 Forrester Research, *Using Digital Channels to Create Breakthrough Multichannel Relationships*, 11 February 2010.

2 Allison Enright, What Amazon's strong growth means for competitors, *Internet Retailer*, October 2010.

3 CMO Council and Catalina Marketing, Losing loyalty: The consumer defection dilemma, 2009.

4 Ibid.

5 CMO Council, *Why Relevance Drives Response and Relationships: Using the power of Precision Marketing to better engage customers*, 2009.

6 CMO Council, The leaders in loyalty: Feeling the love from the loyalty clubs, 2009.

7 CMO Council, *Why Relevance Drives Response and Relationships: Using the power of Precision Marketing to better engage customers*, 2009.

8 Silverpop.com, Email delivery rates above 95%: 16 'must dos' to make it happen, 2009.

9 MediaBUZZ.com, JupiterResearch: Marketers on guard, email marketing facing tough times, November 2008.

10 FTC.gov, *National Do Not Call Registry Data Book for Fiscal Year 2009*.

11 Wikipedia entry: CAN-SPAM Act of 2003 [Online] **http://en.wikipedia.org/wiki/CAN-SPAM_Act_of_2003** and Wikipedia entry: Data Protection Act 1998 [Online] **http://en.wikipedia.org/wiki/Data_Protection_Act_1998**.

12 CMO Council, The leaders in loyalty: Feeling the love from the loyalty clubs, 2009.

13 Julie Katz, *Consumer Interests Drive Email Opens*, Forrester Research, September 2008.

14 Tom Hannigan and Christina Palendrano, Personalization can be quite dynamic, *Information Management*, October 2002.

15 Taos resort trades on tradition, *New Mexico Business Weekly*, February 2006.

16 Laurie Sullivan, BT gets really personal, *Data and Behavioral Insider*, June 2009.

17 Amadesa.com, Case study: Smooth Fitness, May 2009.

18 http://www.royalcanin.ca/

19 Lyris.com, Case study: Royal Canin, 2010.

20 Michael Port and Elizabeth Marshall, *The Contrarian Effect: Why it pays (BIG) to take typical sales advice and do the opposite*, John Wiley, Hoboken, NJ, 2008, p. 37.

21 CMO Council, *The Power of Personalization*, 2008.

22 Jaap Favier, The challenges of CMOs in 2008, Forrester Research, 28 March 2008.

23 Ibid.

24 Don Peppers and Martha Rogers, *The One to One Future*, Currency Doubleday, New York, 1993.

25 CMO Council, *The Power of Personalization*, 2008.

The Precision Marketing Journey

> *There is always free cheese in a mousetrap.*
>
> UNKNOWN

In this chapter, you will learn:

- what to expect on the Precision Marketing journey;

- the steps of the Precision Marketing Framework;

- the questions that each step of the Precision Marketing Framework answers;

- the results companies have achieved by using the Precision Marketing Framework.

Precision Marketing is the ultimate customer-centric approach to marketing and is driven by data-based customer insights and metrics that clearly measure marketing effectiveness. A Precision Marketing approach will help you extract rich and actionable knowledge about your customers. Your customer insights become deepened: you learn what they care about, what motivates them and what causes them to disengage. In return, this information enables you to create meaningful targets and personally relevant content that offers solutions to your customers' needs and helps create long-term, mutually beneficial customer relationships that help maximize ROI.

The value of Precision Marketing is proven across industries, but it is important to keep in mind that the process is a journey. The journey will take time and effort and it will be worth the effort and investment. What can you expect on the journey to Precision Marketing? Let's consider the case of 1-800-Flowers.

The 1-800-Flowers journey

With annual revenue exceeding $700 million and a database of 35 million customers, 1-800-Flowers is now the world's leading florist and gift company. What's impressive about this company, run by brothers Jim and Chris McCann, is their commitment to analytical leadership.

According to the McCanns' recent book *Analytics at Work*, the company's focus on data-driven decision making is a core aspect of its overall approach to strategy. 'We have a culture of analytics and testing,' says Chris McCann, President of 1-800-Flowers. 'I say, "I know what you think – tell me what you can prove."'[1]

Some companies, like 1-800-Flowers, enjoy unprecedented insight into their customers. 'Basically, we know who buys what for what occasion for whom and where it's sent,' said Aaron Cano, Director of Database Marketing at 1-800-Flowers.com.[2] This lets the company build extensive datasets and get to know more about each customer. 1-800-Flowers has the following information on each customer:

- customer name;
- occasion bought for;
- recipient name;
- recipient address;
- channel;
- demographic information.

'Our enterprise data warehouse contains everything from order information to customer name and address to brand and channel IDs, occasions, demographic information from third-party sources, and recipient data,' Cano says.[3]

The company employs its analytical strengths across all of its 11 brands, including Fanny May Confections, The Popcorn Factory and Cheryl & Co. cookies. With these numerous distinct brands, one of the company's core challenges is leveraging its extensive customer data to benefit all of the divisions. Given the company's multiple channels of interaction (retail stores, phone, catalogues and online), analysing all of the company's customer data is an enormous task.

The company has made tremendous strides in dramatically reducing the time it takes to segment customers for a mailer or a catalogue. 'It used to take two or three weeks – now it takes two or three days,' says Aaron Cano, Vice President of Customer Knowledge Management. 'That leaves us time to do more analysis and make sure we're sending relevant offers.'[4]

The marketing team spent years trying to get a handle on all of these data. Marketing was tasked with mapping the data, identifying all possible touchpoints, cleansing the data and recognizing when customers move between sales channels. Working with the SAS Institute, the 1-800-Flowers team was able to construct a custom dashboard and create underlying systems that made key data accessible to employees on demand. 'Previously, business users had to rely on IT to produce monthly reports. Now, they can access and analyze the data themselves at their desktops whenever they want,' says Ron Scala, Director of Information Management for 1-800-Flowers.[5]

The company's loyalty and retention rates are powerful proof that its commitment to data-driven strategies has paid off. In fact, the company has increased its customer retention rate by 10 per cent and increased the retention rate of its best customer segment to more than 80 per cent. The more that 1-800-Flowers engages with its customers in the course of the year, the more likely customers are to discover one of the company's other brands. 'We're successful because it isn't just marketing that buys into the processes,' says Cano. 'Merchandising, fulfillment, operations, and finance all use the customer knowledge to make decisions as well.'[6]

Perhaps most importantly, 1-800-Flowers is leveraging its data to create targeted campaigns and engage its customers in a truly personal fashion. 'It takes a long time for an organization to become analytical,' Cano says. 'But at the end of the day our customers become more loyal to us because we're relevant and we treat them like individuals.'

Deeper data on what customers do – such as how or where they use a product – enable relevance. 'If a customer usually buys tulips for his wife, we show him our newest and best tulip selections,' Cano says.[7]

While providing special offers to customers is not a new concept, the ability to offer customers relevant and targeted promotions that enable a brand to retain customer loyalty across customer touchpoints is new.

As Cano pointed out, Precision Marketing is a multi-step, ongoing and worthwhile journey.

Precision Marketing in perspective

Precision Marketing is about using data-driven insights to deliver the right message to the right person at the right time in the right channel. It is critical to understand that this method involves a data-driven approach, which enables more rational and fact-based marketing decisions. Precision Marketing evolves the marketing practice beyond the realm of relying on mere intuition and gut checks. While experience remains essential to success, it is no longer enough. It is now necessary to gather and analyse all available insight in order to objectively guide your marketing decisions with more depth and precision.

Rather than viewing the customer from the company's perspective, Precision Marketing is about viewing the company, its products and its marketing messages from each customer's perspective. What does the customer want? What does the customer need? Precision Marketing is customer focused, but not in the same way as one-on-one marketing or360-degree marketing. Rather than surround customers from all angles and blast them with messages, Precision Marketing looks at the customer's view of the company.

Do your messages add to the customer's life through information, entertainment, time-critical information or other forms of value to the customer? Are the marketing messages consistent with the goods and services the customer actually wants, chooses and receives? Do your messages arrive when the customer is most receptive and without being intrusive?

The Precision Marketing Framework

Adopting and fully implementing Precision Marketing is not about an instantaneous flip of the switch; it is a journey. This journey is not simple, but it is worthwhile, and your efforts and investments to navigate the journey will reap rewards. In order to guide you through that journey, we have created a Precision Marketing Framework, which includes three major milestones and a series of six steps as depicted in Figure 2.1.

FIGURE 2.1 Six Steps in the Precision Marketing Framework

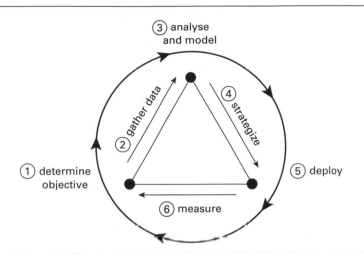

The Precision Marketing Framework, in the simplest terms, is about following a logical, sequential and continually improving process. The framework starts with a business need or objective. It then proceeds through a sequence of tasks and activities, and finally ends with the delivery of measured results. Although we describe the framework in six steps, it is a continuous process practised over and over as refinement and precision are gained over time.

Here are the six steps within our Precision Marketing Framework and the major questions that each step strives to answer:

Step One: Determine your objective

- What specific marketing objectives or business needs are critical to your company's goals?
- What problem are you trying to solve?
- Is your objective measurable, achievable, relevant and timely?
- Here are four popular objectives from which many marketers choose:
    - customer retention;
    - customer growth;
    - customer reactivation;
    - customer acquisition.

Step Two: Gather data

- What customer data will you need?
- From where will you obtain your data?
- What other vehicles will you leverage to gather data?
- The following are possible data sources:
  - internal data;
  - external lists;
  - focus groups;
  - polls and surveys.

Step Three: Analyse and model

- How will you engage your analytics team?
- How will your analytics team utilize the data to generate insights?
- How predictive is your analytics modelling?
- Here are deliverables an analytics team might produce:
  - portfolio analysis;
  - segmentation;
  - industry models;
  - custom algorithms;
  - recommendations.

Step Four: Strategize

- Will you use an existing campaign or create a new one?
- What content and creative will you incorporate into this campaign?
- What offers are you prepared to present?
- What must your message express in order to resonate with your target segment?
- How will you measure your success?
- Your strategy may incorporate one or more of the following delivery channels:
  - direct marketing;
  - e-mail campaigns;
  - banner ads placement;

  - telemarketing;
  - social media;
  - mobile communications.

Step Five: Deploy

- How will you execute your campaign?
- How will you implement the tactics in your selected channels?
- How will you use your data to engage with the targeted customers?

Step Six: Measure

- Did the campaign deliver the anticipated results?
- What did you learn?
- What worked? What did not work?
- What can you improve upon?
- How will you incorporate these findings into your next campaign?

Each of these steps will be described and explained in detail in the following chapters (one step will be described per chapter) to take you through the Precision Marketing Framework. Before we begin, we would like to share with you our first publicized implementation of Precision Marketing to demonstrate its power. Although our first implementation of Precision Marketing might seem basic, the results are compelling. As a part of a partnership with Best Western, we redesigned their loyalty statement to increase customer engagement, drive customer loyalty and generate incremental revenue. As you will see, this first basic step was able to generate significant returns for Best Western. This is now one of many compelling testimonies demonstrating the power of Precision Marketing.

Best practices at Best Western

Best Western International, founded in 1946 by veteran California hotelier MK Guertin, hosts 400,000 guests worldwide each night. Today, 'The World's Largest Hotel Chain®' is 66 years young and operates as a non-profit, member association hotelier, meaning that all of its more than 4,000 locations in 80 countries are independently owned and operated.

'A lot of companies find themselves doing the same things over and over. At Best Western, we definitely test new marketing ideas to see what moves the needle,' says Tammy Lucas, Managing Director of Marketing Programs, Best Western International.[8] According to Lucas, Best Western Rewards members represent some of their most active and invested customers. 'Our rewards statements have typically been reporting rather than response vehicles,' Lucas says. 'With the help of InfoPrint and the CMO Council, we identified ways to expand our interaction with customers.'[9]

Best Western, always interested in innovation and fresh ideas, was open to testing new types of marketing tactics which could grow and enhance customer loyalty. Partnering with us at Ricoh, two companies decided to run a campaign that would be delivered to Best Western Rewards members through a redesigned loyalty statement. The purpose of this trial was to increase revenue through incremental bookings and grow awareness for the hotel's co-branded credit card. Best Western was also looking for a way to promote its new loyalty programme, 'More Rewards, Faster,' which helped its members earn double points or miles if they booked stays during a set period of time.

With a deadline of only four weeks for complete campaign implementation and execution, all stakeholders had to quickly agree on the campaign strategy. Internal Best Western divisions, such as marketing and IT, as well as outside partners (which included the design firms, loyalty partner programmes, the print providers and Ricoh) needed to quickly collaborate on the creative, data requirements, metrics and timelines to meet the deadline for the autumn promotion.

As Best Western and Ricoh launched this campaign, the delivery of relevant messaging was foremost in the thoughts of executives of both companies. The InfoPrint Data Analytics Practice assisted with the needed analysis to ensure the delivery of relevant messaging. Using basic business rule data analysis (if/then testing), the Data Analytics Practice was able to identify which reward members would receive an offer for the co-branded Best Western MasterCard and which members already had one and thus would receive a reminder to use it.

The campaign included two statistically equivalent groups of 50,000 each. The first 50,000 members served as the test group receiving the old statement, and the second 50,000 received the redesigned statement with customized offers.

This promotion was completed and delivered on time, during the autumn of 2008. The results were scheduled for measurement four weeks after the launch. Unfortunately, neither company expected what was about to happen in the US market. The promotion for travel and credit was received by Best Western's loyalty members the same week the US stock market crashed. Both companies were left hoping for the best but anticipating a lacklustre campaign. The results were measured four weeks after the campaign launched, as scheduled, and the results were delivered to the Data Analytics Practice for processing.

The results were impressive, especially considering the economic turmoil taking place at the time: the test group earned a 278 per cent return on investment (Figure 2.2). This 278 per cent ROI was achieved by implementing the Precision Marketing Framework. As the Precision Marketing Framework prescribed, we determined the objective for the campaign, gathered and analysed customer data to segment customers and create a relevant offer, strategized the campaign and delivery channel, deployed it and measured the results. The results delivered an almost twofold increase in Best Western's ROI metric. The uptick in performance was related to an increase in the revenue line as more individuals responded in conjunction with a decrease in the expense line related to the reduced use of paper. An indirect benefit was that the new statement design represented a 40 per cent decrease in the use of paper, providing a significant green benefit. Thus, Best Western proved that it could produce superior results while contributing to greater environmental sustainability.

FIGURE 2.2 Best Western ROI Results

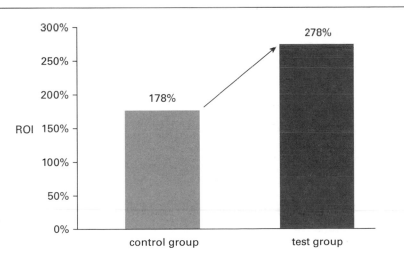

Best Western's objectives of increasing revenue through incremental bookings, growing awareness for the hotel's co-branded credit card and launching its 'More Rewards, Faster' campaign proved successful. In addition to generating a triple-digit ROI, the company also realized the following:

- 39% lift over the control group for number of stays;
- 34% lift over the control group for number of nights stayed;
- 30% lift over control for revenue generated;
- 500% lift over the control group applying for the Best Western Rewards MasterCard.

Another unexpected finding was the significant savings associated with moving from inserts to onserts. The Ricoh team incorporated the direct mail pieces that had previously been 'inserted' in the envelope into the design of the statement. This enabled the marketing team to substantially reduce paper expenses, which contributed to the campaign's ROI. Further, the saving in paper is beneficial to businesses looking for ways to reduce their environmental footprint without compromising their profitability or undermining business objectives.

The most important result was a 15 per cent uptick in the response rate. While the above findings were impressive, none of them would have occurred had customers not responded to the relevant information, registered for the promotional programme and thus engaged with the brand. Relevant content, delivered in a clearly defined statement, drove customers to engage. 'We are delighted in the results of this trial and our work with the CMO Council and Ricoh,' Lucas says. 'This pilot really does underline our ongoing commitment to rewarding our loyal customers and our commitment to continually deepen our relationships with them.' This uptick, while the smallest number in the group, is the most significant because it addresses the fundamentals of Precision Marketing.

Take the Precision Marketing journey

Adopting an analytical approach to your business and marketing practices – which we term Precision Marketing – is a multi-step, evolutionary journey. You can begin to realize improving and impressive returns with simple steps forward using the Precision Marketing Framework. In each of the customer implementations in which we have been involved, not a single customer or business has chosen to abandon the Framework after having learned it. We believe that these rewards are available to all businesses willing to take the steps and begin the journey. As we'll discuss in the next chapter, the first step, 'Determine Your Objective', will start the Precision Marketing journey. Let's begin.

Key takeaway messages from Chapter 2, 'The Precision Marketing Journey'

- Precision Marketing is a journey. It is not a simple journey, but it is worthwhile and your efforts and investments to navigate the journey will reap rich rewards.

- The six steps of the journey, outlined in the Precision Marketing Framework, are:
  1 Step One: Determine Your Objective;
  2 Step Two: Gather Data;
  3 Step Three: Analyse and Model;
  4 Step Four: Strategize;
  5 Step Five: Deploy;
  6 Step Six: Measure.

- The Precision Marketing journey in action at 1-800-Flowers:
  1 Step One: Objective: to improve customer retention.
  2 Step Two: Gather Data. The company gathered data such as customer name, occasion bought for, recipient name, recipient address, channel, demographic info.
  3 Step Three: Analyse and Model. The company analysed and modelled data across its 11 brands and multiple channels of interaction (retail stores, phone catalogues and online).
  4 Step Four: Strategize. The company decided to segment customers into multiple categories, determine its best customers and drill down to the individual level to create special offers tailored to specific individuals.
  5 Step Five: Deploy. The company created a custom dashboard that lets employers access and analyse data across all customers and touchpoints to recognize when customers move between sales channels and brands;
  6 Step Six: Measure. Given the company's goal of customer retention, the company chose to track retention among all its customers and also among its best customers. The results achieved from Precision Marketing were an increase in overall customer retention rate of 10%, and the retention rate of its best customer segment increased more than 80%.

- The Precision Marketing journey in action at Best Western:

  1 Step One: Objectives. The company's objectives were to increase revenue through incremental bookings, promote loyalty and build awareness of the hotel chain's co-branded credit card.

  2 Step Two: Gather Data. The company used internal data to create two statistically equivalent groups of 50,000 customers each.

  3 Step Three: Analyse and Model. The company modelled customers along the following dimensions: number of hotel stays per customer, whether the customer was a member of the loyalty programme, whether the customer had the Best Western credit card, and the total revenue per customer.

  4 Step Four: Strategize. The company decided to run a campaign that would be delivered to its loyalty programme members through a redesigned loyalty statement.

  5 Step Five: Deploy. The company deployed the campaign to 100,000 customers during the autumn of 2008.

  6 Step Six: Measure. On the basis of its objectives, the company set its metrics to measure revenue increases per customer, and whether a customer obtained the new credit card or used it if he or she already had one. The company also measured the response rate and the ROI of the campaign. The results were a 39% lift over the control group for number of stays, a 34% lift over the control group for number of nights stayed, a 30% lift over control for revenue generated, a 500% lift over the control group applying for the Best Western Rewards MasterCard, a 15% uptick in response rate, and triple-digit ROI.

Notes

1 Thomas Davenport, Jeanne Harris and Robert Morison, *Analytics at Work*, Harvard Business School Press, Boston, MA, 2010.

2 From data to dollar$, *1to1 Magazine*, 23 February 2009.

3 Ibid.

4 SAS.com, Case study: 1-800-Flowers, 2010.

5 Ibid.

6 Ibid.

7 Ibid.

8 Best Western melds old and new, *Response Magazine*, March 2009.

9 Ibid.

Step One: Determine Your Objective

> *The will to win is meaningless without the will to prepare.*
>
> SIR WINSTON CHURCHILL

In this chapter, you will learn:

- the four most popular objectives that marketers choose for their Precision Marketing campaigns;
- five secondary objectives that companies can choose;
- how to get organizational alignment on your objectives;
- the key to effective objectives.

Precision Marketing is a journey. As with most journeys, knowing your final destination is the key to being able to map out the direction and details of the journey. For Precision Marketing, it is the same: the first step is to clearly determine and articulate your objective. Let's start with an example to demonstrate Step One in practice by taking a look at what Rogers Wireless has done.

Rogers Wireless executes to reach highly targeted segments

FIGURE 3.1 Rogers Wireless Overview

Rogers Wireless	
Objective:	Improve customer retention and increase customer acquisition
Strategy:	Produce new customer segments and increase relevance in communications
Tactics:	Double number of campaigns with fewer targets, home in on customer targets and create highly relevant messages
Results:	Moved from 40 lists to 200 more targeted customer lists, increased marketing productivity without increasing headcount, created a data analytics department

One company that is fully capitalizing on customer insight is Rogers Wireless, Canada's leading provider of mobile communication services. The company, which has relied on Precision Marketing approaches to remain competitive and keep pace with its demanding customers, has executed highly targeted marketing campaigns addressed to increasingly focused customer segments. As a result of such efforts, the company has doubled the number of campaigns it produces monthly while improving its marketing results.

To drive success in Canada's hyper-competitive wireless services market, Rogers Wireless is challenged to not only attract new customers but also retain its existing ones. Rogers must offer rate plans and mobile phones that are priced competitively, as well as new plans for smartphones. By diligently analysing its customer base using tools from SAS, the company can determine how best to target its customers with relevant messages. 'Nothing irritates customers more than receiving marketing messages for something that's completely irrelevant to them,' says Derek Pollitt, Director of

Campaign Management and Customer Analysis for Rogers Wireless. He adds that the company's analytical efforts help ensure 'there's a statistically high likelihood that a customer will be interested in an offer.'[1]

Using data warehouses that contain call detail records and subscriber data, the company's statisticians have been able to support marketers to produce insight-driven campaigns. They have leveraged sophisticated analytical tools to produce specific offers for targeted customer groups without increasing marketing headcount. 'We used to have to work overtime just to get 40 customer lists out each month,' says Pollitt. 'Now we regularly send out more than 200 lists, which are smaller and more targeted.'[2]

The company's efforts have increased response rates while enhancing the performance of staff members. Some team members have even evolved from list pullers to campaign analysts, enabling Rogers Wireless to 'be more targeted and more relevant to the customer so we can stay ahead of our competition,' Pollitt says.

The company's analytical tools and deepening skills have also paid off in terms of overall productivity and efficiency. 'We're more efficient and more effective and, as a result, a lot happier,' says Pollitt. 'And we can dig deeper into our mountains of data, rather than just skim across the top.'[3]

It is extraordinary what Rogers Wireless has been able to achieve using the principles of the Precision Marketing Framework. Rogers' clear-cut objectives enabled the company to take bold steps in moving from 40 to 200 campaigns a month with smaller, more precise customer targeting. Leveraging its insights resulted in impressive returns back to the business. Rogers' clarity and commitment to its objectives continue to provide the foundation for its Precision Marketing journey.

Getting started

As with all journeys, what is most important is to get started. Let's take a look at our first milestone, which is Step One: Determine Your Objective.

FIGURE 3.2 Step One of Precision Marketing Framework

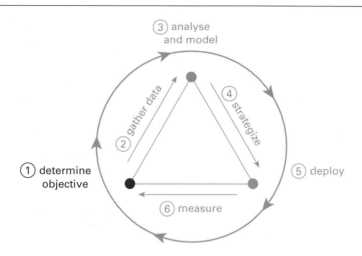

Determining your objective

Setting a clear and measurable objective is the foundational step that creates the parameters for your journey through a Precision Marketing implementation. What is the problem you are trying to solve? What are the key pain points your company is experiencing? If you start with exceptional clarity in this first stage, you will be in a strong position to deliver valuable, measurable and meaningful results.

Unfortunately, many falter at this stage. Marketers are reluctant to stray from old, comfortable habits. Advertising agencies provide high-level reporting back on the often uninformative metrics. Others will use 'spray and pray' tactics, hoping to achieve success by playing the saturation game. Most of these efforts fail because the objectives set were too broad and the measurements too vague or too few.

Instead, here are four popular objectives from which marketers can choose:

1 customer retention;

2 customer growth;

3 customer reactivation;

4 customer acquisition.

Objective 1: customer retention

Customer retention revolves around keeping or retaining your existing customers. Research suggests that it may cost seven times more to acquire a new customer than to retain and grow an existing customer. The cost and time savings of customer retention as against acquisition are key reasons to place a high priority on understanding the behaviours of your best customers.

Until now, only large companies have had the toolsets and financial resources necessary to implement a disciplined customer retention strategy or a way to identify their most valuable customers. In the past, smaller companies may have perceived customer retention programmes as costly and expensive to maintain, yet larger companies realized that losing existing customers is even more costly and potentially more devastating to a company's bottom line.

Today, new technology is widely available and affordable, offering all types of businesses, large or small, the tools and resources necessary to grow their understanding of customer behaviours and anticipate their wants and needs. Using these technologies, companies are able to leverage rich insights from customer data in order to put the valued customer at the centre of their retention marketing programme.

Data are 'an essential part of customer revenue optimization and life-time value building,' said Donovan Neale-May, Founder and Executive Director of the CMO Council. The goal is to know who your best customers are, cut through the messaging turmoil and make all your communications and touchpoints with your best customers highly relevant. Relevancy is the new route to revenue.

How Fiat used data to improve customer retention by more than 6 per cent

FIGURE 3.3 Fiat Overview

Fiat	
Objective:	Improve customer retention
Strategy:	Grow understanding of the brand, and dealer actions, and improve online marketing activities
Tactics:	Gathered data through surveying existing and prospective customers, purchased third-party data on behaviour
Results:	6% improvement

The Italian car maker Fiat Group wanted to improve customer retention. To do this, Fiat first collected survey data from existing and prospective customers and then bought third-party data on car purchasing behaviour, such as data on how often people replace their cars. Then Fiat used software from SPSS to mine these data to:

1 predict customers' responses to the brand;

2 predict dealer actions;

3 create effective online marketing activities.

'The main focus is how to be effective in managing the data and the brands,' said Giovanni Lux, Customer Intelligence Manager for Fiat. The results? Using the data and modelling, Fiat made changes that improved customer retention by over 6 per cent. Overall, 54 per cent of Fiat owners buy another Fiat when they replace their car.[4]

Objective: customer growth

Many marketers understand that the fastest and most cost-efficient way of growing revenue is up-selling and cross-selling to their existing customer base. For example, in the insurance industry it is a well-known fact that customers having two or more related insurance products are much less likely to switch insurance companies than customers who have only one product. In addition, our research on the insurance industry has indicated that customers who have two or more products are loyal to the provider for 5 to 10 years longer than those customers who only use one product.[5]

Growing your existing customers by up-selling and cross-selling services and products is the best way to increase loyalty and ultimately contribute to current profitability. The way to achieve precision in customer growth is to determine which customer should receive which offer, or what customer segment would want to know about a particular product. Recall the poll conducted by the CMO Council, which found that over 73 per cent of consumers were receiving offers for products they had already purchased.[6] Not only is that a costly waste of a company's marketing budget, but it also negatively impacts the brand and leads to defection from the brand.

Many marketers understand the advantages of cross-selling and up-selling to existing customers to grow relationships and revenue, and build loyalty. However, few marketers understand the logic behind predicting customers' needs and providing the right offer at the time of conversion. This prediction requires precision.

Greetings from American Greetings

FIGURE 3.4 American Greetings Overview

American Greetings
Objectives: Customer growth Increase e-card purchases and online subscriptions from existing customer base
Strategy: Leverage insight gained by data-mining activities on card preferences to grow revenue from existing base
Tactics: E-mail campaign to different segments to promote sentiment or humour. Implement a test and control group
Results: 70% increase in conversions

Understanding what is relevant to each customer requires marketers to look at their customer data, allowing precise segmentation of the customer base in order to determine which segments will produce the most beneficial customer insights. From these insights, marketers can then determine the relevant offers to deliver to each segment. Many company-centric marketers may consider customer data, such as demographics, to be a tried-and-true source. However, in many cases the truly significant data that affect the customization of marketing messages are unique to the industry – such as how different customers select offers, perceive value, or use the product. These differences often determine which marketing message will be most relevant to that customer.

Consider American Greetings, the greetings card company, which wanted to encourage more e-card purchases and annual subscriptions by e-mailing its customers. A generic message for card-sending customers would be about as appealing as a generic birthday card. If a greetings card is supposed to resonate with the recipient, then American Greetings needed to ensure that the greeting to its customers would resonate, too.

American Greetings looked at a number of variables, including historical greetings card purchases, and noticed an important pattern related to traditional demographic variables. The company found that some people love traditional sentimental greetings cards that tug the heartstrings, while others enjoy humorous cards that make them laugh. American Greetings created e-mail messages geared to both preferences. The company then sent the greetings card on the basis of customers' past purchase activities. The intelligently segmented and targeted messages produced a 70 per cent improvement in conversion rates when compared to the control group.

Objective: customer reactivation

Customer reactivation is another objective that companies might choose to pursue. In this objective, marketers recognize the potential of their past customers to re-engage with the brand. Alternatively, marketers can leverage historical buying behaviours to learn more about potential new customers.

A large, costly and little-known mistake is when companies ignore (or even write off) customers who have not engaged in a recent transaction. Many companies do not bother to market to these dormant customers; they assume the customers have defected or lost interest. As a result, the historical data go untouched and unvalued and are often categorized as 'dead data.'

The truth is that enormous – and unrealized – gains can be reaped by reaching out to inactive customers and re-engaging them with relevant and timely offers to convert those customers from inactive to engaged customers once again. In order to create the relevant offers, it is necessary to mine and leverage the rich (and often discarded) insights that lie within historical data sources.

How Perricone MD uses 'inactive' customer lists

FIGURE 3.5 Perricone MD Overview

Perricone MD	
Objective:	Re-engage dormant customers
Strategy:	Reconnect with dormant customers with frequent relevant messages and offers
Tactics:	Send e-mails, samples and discount offers
Results:	33% of inactive customers responded

One common list is the so-called 'dead list' of customers who have not bought from the company for a while but who have not actively disengaged by unsubscribing. Consider the case of Perricone MD, a high-end skin care company founded by Dr Nicholas Perricone.[7] The company had thousands of people who had opted in to Perricone MD's mailing list but had stopped responding to the company's messages. Instead of continuing to blast these people with the same messages as those sent to active customers, Perricone MD crafted a special campaign to encourage re-engagement. It sent weekly offers of low-priced sample sizes or sale prices of full-sized products encouraging its drop-out customers to buy a little just to try the product.

Perricone's results prove that companies should not despair over past irrelevancies. Even if marketers sent irrelevant messaging in the past, they can become relevant and regain credibility by providing more personal attention. Perricone's results: 33 per cent of the inactive customers responded to Perricone's messages, and 5,000 of them went on to make at least two purchases. 'It's much cheaper to re-engage a customer than it is to get a new one,' says Neil Kjeldsen, Vice-President of E-Commerce for Perricone MD.

'Even if they don't buy with the same level of intensity as the "good" list, they're still buying, and we're able to show growth.'

Objective: customer acquisition

Acquiring new customers poses a real relevance puzzler. First, companies know the least about prospective new customers. By definition, they haven't bought anything from the company yet, so there is a dearth of data on them. Second, these prospective customers may be the most demanding when it comes to relevance because they may prefer other companies and be reluctant to switch to a new company. Existing customers already know who the company is, what it does and why they've bought from the company in the past. New customers do not know the company. Thus, the company needs to be especially relevant and engaging in that first impression. The key to solving this puzzle and unlocking the value of new customers is to find available data on prospective customers and use those data to match and model prospective customers to existing customers.

Clearly, new customer acquisition is an important objective for marketers. As in the customer reactivation example above, it is crucial to understand your current customer's behaviours, preferences and needs and then apply those insights and attributes to your prospective customer acquisition list. Let's look at how Rapid Racking did this.

How Rapid Racking reduced cost per acquired customer by 47 per cent

FIGURE 3.6 Rapid Racking Overview

Rapid Racking	
Objective:	Customer acquisition at a reduced cost
Strategy:	How to use data to create better relevance for prospecting new customers
Tactics:	Deliver fewer mailings of smaller catalogues to more targeted prospects
Results:	Costs reduced by 47% while revenue increased by 8%

In the past, Rapid Racking, a UK-based maker of shelving and racking for businesses, blasted out millions of copies of its 160-page product catalogues to any potential shelving buyer inside every imaginable business. The company knew it needed to reduce customer acquisition costs. And yet, Rapid Racking didn't want to give up on new customers and only market to its existing customers. New customers are often the key to new growth horizons.[8]

Rapid Racking looked at how to use data to reduce costs by creating better relevance for prospective customers. The company's marketers looked at the data they could collect on the prospects – such as job title and job responsibility – and then used current in-house data on existing customers to predict which prospects were the most promising. This let Rapid Racking cut the number of pieces mailed by almost 25 per cent.

The company also used the data to increase the relevance and decrease the costs of each mailing by creating more targeted, less expensive mini-catalogues. Every quarter, the company now buys third-party data on prospects in the B2B space and uses third-party software to craft a smaller mailing of smaller catalogues. Instead of mailing 4 million massive catalogues to everyone, Rapid Racking mails only 250,000 large catalogues and about 3 million mini-catalogues to a more targeted set of prospects. The result? A 47 per cent decrease in the cost per acquired customer while maintaining an 8 per cent rate of revenue growth.[9]

Other tactical objectives

Although acquisition, retention and cross-selling are the dominant strategic objectives for marketing, companies might also pursue other tactical objectives such as cost reduction. The Rapid Racking example, in addition to illustrating customer acquisition, also illustrates the broader principle that Precision Marketing makes your company smarter, and that means you can reduce costs. Traditional imprecise marketing can be very expensive in the short term because of spray-and-pray attempts to reach people through brute force. Data and the opportunities for relevance that data creates can reduce the costs of marketing and other functions by enabling you:

- to know each customer well enough that you don't send messages that will be irrelevant;
- to know each customer so that you send shorter, less costly messages that include only relevant content;

- to know each customer so you can provide better service that reduces product returns and complaints.

Companies can also use Precision Marketing for other tactical objectives such as:

- ensuring prompt payment of invoices;
- migration to online self-service channels;
- completion of a customer profile;
- participation in a customer survey.

Organizational alignment on objectives

Although much of Precision Marketing primarily concerns precision on the customer side, another element of successful Precision Marketing is in the precision of fit to the company. In particular, the objectives of a Precision Marketing campaign need to precisely fit the broader strategies of the company. That means considering how marketing objectives roll up into company-wide strategic objectives such as new market entry, revenue expansion, channel strategies or cost-reduction strategies.

In addition, once a company has a marketing objective it may need tighter coordination between marketing and other functions to achieve that objective. For example, France Telecom, the number one provider of broadband internet services in Europe and the number three mobile operator, wanted to retain customers and grow revenues per customer. Achieving those objectives affected not only what the company said but also what it sold. 'A product that is not market- and consumer-relevant does not strengthen the brand,' says Jean-Philippe Vanot, Senior Executive Vice President of Innovation and Marketing for France Telecom.

France Telecom combined the marketing organization and R&D organization to align the two functions. 'One of the first moves I made when I took over the innovation and marketing organization was to create a single, unified design and development team that includes both R&D and marketing,' says Vanot. The tools that make Precision Marketing work can also aid product development. '[We use] more sophisticated analytics and recommendation tools to analyze all the customer usage data coming in, and then use that data to provide more personalized and customized services,' Vanot concluded. 'Different parts of our company now can come together to work toward the common goal of customer-centric offerings.'[10]

The keys to effective objectives

The first step of the Precision Marketing Framework, 'Determine Your Objective', is the most critical step. Clearly defined objectives are key not only for the success of this step but to the entire Precision Marketing implementation.

Objectives should be very specific, time based, measurable, relevant and achievable in order to support your corporate goal. Measurements are an important aspect of your objectives because they numerically gauge your performance on executing the objectives. As we have seen in the cases of American Greeting Cards, Fiat, Rapid Racking and Perricone MD, aligning the right objective to the right strategy and implementing the right tactics generate a clear and measurable return back to each of the businesses.

The Precision Marketing Framework follows a process that begins with a clearly identified business need or objective that is in line with corporate goals. The next step, number two in the Framework, moves us from Determine Your Objective to Gather Data. Step Two involves collecting data from both internal and external sources to validate the objectives established in Step One.

FIGURE 3.7 The Precision Marketing Framework

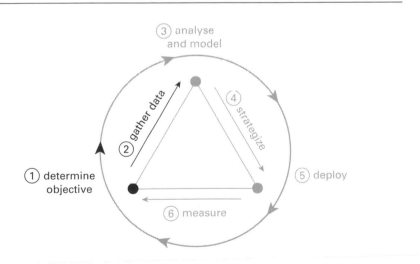

> Key takeaway messages from Chapter 3, 'Step One: Determine Your Objective'
>
> - Step One of the Precision Marketing journey is to determine your objective. Step One answers the question: what is the problem you are trying to solve? Four potential problems areas to solve are:
>   - customer retention: keeping your current customers;
>   - customer growth: growing your current customers;
>   - customer reactivation: reactivating dormant customers;
>   - customer acquisition: acquiring new customers.
>
>   These are the four most popular objectives from which companies choose.
>
> - Marketing objectives must align with organization-wide strategic objectives.
>
> - Companies can also pursue secondary objectives that help them save money or learn more about a customer.
>
> - The key to effective objectives is to make them specific, time-based and measurable.

Notes

1 SAS, SAS® helps Rogers Wireless get personal with customers [Online] **http://www.sas.com/success/Rogers.html**.

2 Ibid.

3 Ibid.

4 Tim Ferguson, Businesses hunting for gold with data mining, 18 May 2009 [Online] **http://www.zdnetasia.com/businesses-hunting-for-gold-with-data-mining-62054105.htm**.

5 CMO Council, *What's Critical in the Vertical – Insurance*, 2010.

6 CMO Council, *Why Relevance Drives Relationships and Response*, 2009.

7 Kimberly Smith, Case study: Reviving the dead list to grow email revenues [Online] **http://www.marketingprofs.com/casestudy/146**.

8 AllBusiness.com, Case study: Rapid Racking finds its focus [Online] **http://www.allbusiness.com/reports-reviews-sections/case-studies/12165457-1.html**.

9 Ibid.

10 Accenture, France Telecom: growth and innovation: an interview with Jean-Philippe Vanot, *Outlook Q&A*, November 2009 [Online] **http://www.accenture.com/SiteCollectionDocuments/ PDF/Accenture_OutlookQA_FranceTelecom_Nov09.pdf.**

Step Two: Gather Data

In this chapter, you will learn:

- the role of data in Precision Marketing;

- the four barriers to getting internal data;

- sources and ways to get data;

- best practices relating to data use;

- how to use locational data;

- how to use polls and surveys to get data;

- how to use free-form data.

Looking for a way to level the playing field with a larger competitor? Or are you looking for ways to stay ahead of your smaller and more nimble rivals? Either way, your data may prove to be your most powerful weapon in this hyper-competitive era, particularly if you can apply rigour and discipline to that data. Let's look at the example of Oakland Athletics (known as the Oakland A's) to see how it works.

FIGURE 4.1 Oakland A's Overview

Oakland A's	
Objective:	Create a winning team with a small budget
Strategy:	Develop an analytics model to determine which undervalued players were going to produce for them. Analyse the data to make the most of their investments
Tactics:	Hire a data analyst to recognize and create new methodologies
	Analyse the statistics in new ways
	Acquire the undervalued players
Results:	Built an affordable team of underrated players to make it to the play-offs in 5 of 10 years to create a measurable return on their investment

In his best-selling book (now made into a film) *Moneyball: The Art Of Winning An Unfair Game*, Michael Lewis told the story of Oakland's baseball team under the leadership of Billy Beane. The book discusses how an organization can develop effective, fresh strategies by looking at data in innovative ways. It demonstrates how you can literally change the game by competing with analytics.

Beane proved that one of the league's most underfunded teams could consistently win games and secure a position in the post-season play-offs. With a payroll one-third the size of that of many teams in the league, the A's reached the play-offs for four consecutive years, an extraordinary feat that left many scratching their heads. 'At the bottom of the Oakland experiment,' writes Lewis, 'was a willingness to rethink baseball: how it is managed, how it is played, who is best suited to play it, and why.'

While other teams paid top dollar for star power, the Oakland team identified which players were undervalued by crunching the numbers and analysing the statistics in new ways. This helped the team recruit and acquire effective performers for a fraction of what others paid. The team also re-examined conventional baseball statistics and identified hidden inefficiencies in the game that could be exploited to achieve success. Most importantly, the team proved that rigorous analytical capabilities could be employed to outsmart and outcompete rivals who were much better financed.

The counter-intuitive insights behind the A's winning strategy were traceable to a man named Bill James. Having studied literature and economics at the University of Kansas, James first began writing down his thoughts about baseball as a nightwatchman at a Stokely-Van Camp pork and beans factory. In his self-published 1977 *Baseball Abstract: Featuring 18 categories of statistical information that you just can't find anywhere else*, James first began challenging the statistical assumptions at the heart of baseball.

Conventional statistics, as James saw it, were profoundly misleading, and each year he would publish a new abstract confronting the conventional wisdom. He was challenging everything from fielding errors to 'runs batted in', claiming that they were poor measures of a player's true value. One of James' most significant arguments was that 'on base percentage' was a superior metric to batting average. As he saw it, a walk – which had no impact on a player's batting average – was as important as a single. After all, both got you to first base and three bags closer to a run. With player salaries climbing dramatically over the years, the potential value of James' analysis rose.

James was not alone. Amateur enthusiasts of all kinds – think tank statisticians, government economists and even a research scientist at a large pharmaceutical company – were now hooked on baseball analysis. They were all making smart contributions to the study of baseball statistics, which came to be known as 'Sabermetrics'. They were mining the data and making sense of them, identifying new patterns. Big-league baseball insiders, however, paid them no heed.

It was not until Billy Beane was named general manager of the Oakland A's in 1997 that the insights of James and other outsiders were truly applied. Beane was a huge fan of James' *Baseball Abstract*, mentioned earlier, and embraced the arguments of that book. Beane strongly believed that traditional metrics were failing the game of baseball and that statistical data could tell a story about a player's potential that baseball scouts simply could not.

Determined to challenge the status quo, Beane decided his first recruit would be a statistician. He chose Paul dePodesta, a Harvard graduate with a keen interest in the connections between psychology and economics. Laptop in hand, dePodesta would crunch data on players and potential strategies. He would generate new hypotheses and then proceed to run statistical tests and experiments.

On the basis of this analysis, the A's would recruit players overlooked by major league scouts and play the game in ways other teams would not. 'Plate discipline' (the practice of learning which pitches to swing for the best game outcome), which could draw a walk, was a highly prized skill among

A's batters, enabling the A's to move players into the optimal scoring positions. The team would actively focus on 'manufacturing runs' by making sacrifice bunts (meaning that the batter holds the bat in the hitting zone and allows the ball to make contact with it but merely deadens the ball without attempting to strike it forcefully) that moved players into scoring positions.

Why sacrifice bunts? Bunts can help win ball games, and the A's trusted their data and planned their strategies by aligning their business objectives with the data analysis to create winning tactics. As the A's began winning pennants at a remarkable rate, others took notice.

In the years to follow, the New York Mets, New York Yankees, San Diego Padres, Boston Red Sox and Toronto Blue Jays have all hired full-time Sabermetric analysts. The game of baseball has changed. The power of data analysis as a force for strategic decision making and a lever for successful action is now thoroughly embedded in major league baseball.

It wasn't a difficult walk in the business of baseball for the owners and general managers to embrace the importance of new and interesting ways of using statistics. Many companies are in a similar analytical position: they have used their historical data, now they need to recognize and embrace the new methodologies to use data to achieve their business goals and advance into the future.

The *Moneyball* story reflects a wider trend, one that is reshaping business and marketing by demonstrating the incredible power and rich potential that data represent. Whether your company is large or small, a market leader or a market challenger, data are fast becoming your most powerful competitive weapon. And your competitive edge is relevance.

Now that we have completed Step One and determined our objective, we will proceed to Step Two and gather data. In order to take this step, you will need to understand and gather the data that are available.

The latent power of leveraging data is still a widely missed concept in business, especially in the marketing department. However, the mandate to leverage data is no longer an option, it's a must-do, and the powerful insights that data enable will reap rewards for marketers who choose to embrace it in the years ahead.

FIGURE 4.2 Step 2 of Precision Marketing Framework

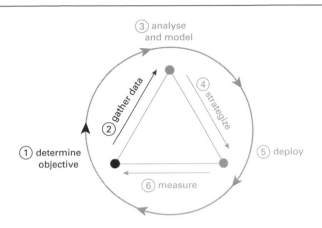

The role of data in Precision Marketing

In this new era of customer power, companies create relevance and revenues by focusing on the customer. Precision Marketing is about bonding, not branding. While branding marketers communicate with more of a 'shout' at the market about how great their company and products are, Precision Marketers converse with their customer about what their customers want and then show how their offerings or products satisfy those needs.

Data enable customer insights. Customer insights drive relevance. Most marketers collect what is easy rather than what is insightful. Precision Marketers collect data that allow for a deeper customer understanding. These data let them create relevant marketing campaigns and strategies tailored to the customers' needs. Companies already collect quite a large number of data. In fact, the CMO Council found that nearly 73 per cent collect basic demographics and 67.5 per cent track the location of members.[1]

Yet too many companies just aggregate their data without trying to know customers in greater detail. 'Relevant data continues to be a limiting factor in customer engagement,' says Donovan Neale-May of the CMO Council. The CMO Council found that very few marketers leverage the valuable customer insights such as:

- advocacy rates (14.3%);
- brand loyalty and attachment (27.1%);
- personal preferences (31.4%);

- satisfaction levels (33%);
- product preferences (37.8%).[2]

As a result, marketers miss knowledge about their customers that they could have had. 'Without a deeper customer insight, marketers will be limited in their ability to do meaningful predictive modeling, market segmentation and revenue forecasting,' Neale-May continues.[3] 'If a marketer doesn't have the access to that [relevant] data, to do the analysis to see where key behaviors are beginning and ending or where key attributes are, then it can't build out campaigns to be relevant,' says Ben Ardito, Vice President of Professional Services at e-Dialog (an e-mail services provider).[4]

Yet this knowledge gap also implies a big opportunity. 'Better understanding of customer behaviors, predispositions, intentions and preferences enables more effective and relevant messaging,' Neale-May says.[5] By collecting data to create relevance, marketers gain a real opportunity to leapfrog the competition.

Data increase the value of a business. The perceived value of a company's data is between 37 per cent and 40 per cent of the total value of the entire company, according to a PricewaterhouseCoopers study.[6] As marketing is redefined, so too are other aspects within a company. As underscored by this PricewaterhouseCoopers study, the power of data is emerging as a significant and leverageable asset within a business.

Getting to your internal data

FIGURE 4.3 Senior marketers who realize the full potential of customers

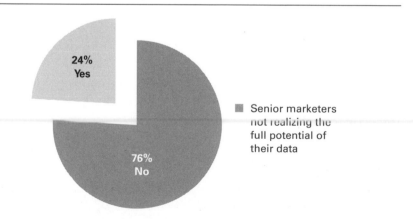

24%
Yes

76%
No

Senior marketers not realizing the full potential of their data

Despite the depressed global economy going into 2012, a surprising 76 per cent of senior marketers surveyed believe they are not realizing the full revenue potential of their current customers.[7] They are leaving money on the table by not gathering data on their customers. In addition, only 46.5 per cent say they have good insights into retention rates, customer profitability and lifetime value. This provides a significant upside opportunity for marketers to originate programmes that create immediate business value.

The CMO Council's audit of some 650 senior marketers revealed that making communications more personal and relevant, as well as more targeted and timely, was among the top strategies for realizing greater revenue and profitability from existing customers. Other leading strategies included addressing under-penetrated markets or new customer segments, as well as finding new ways to up-sell and cross-sell existing accounts.

The CMO Council study highlighted three key obstacles and deficiencies for not optimizing the full revenue potential and lifetime value of existing customers:

- Lack of real-time data and analytics to capture insights from all customer touchpoints.
- Information being not only selectively gathered but also often inaccurate or incomplete.
- Data being siloed and restricted in their availability for study and use across the organization.

These findings were a surprise considering the economic situation at the time, but siloing of data has posed problems for marketing teams for several years. Typically, the reasons for these data barriers fall into four categories:

- inaccessibility;
- incomprehensibility;
- inaccuracy;
- inability to act.

Inaccessibility

There is often an organizational chasm between the people who manage data and the people who require the use of those data in order to take action. These two disparate groups often have different priorities, incentives and even professional vocabularies.

In many cases, departments outside of marketing have the responsibility to manage the data as well as the infrastructure that captures that data. Very often, information is stored in databases that are virtually inaccessible to marketers. Even internal analytics teams may not have access to the data.

Incomprehensibility

Even when accessibility and visibility are viable for internal data, marketers may not have enough documentation on the existing data to have a clear understanding of their value or meaning. In fact, there may be such a quantity of data available that it is difficult to sort through what is valuable and what is not.

Very often, the root cause is not that data are lacking, but rather that the organization is lacking the skill set to interpret the existing data. If the necessary skills do not exist in your organization, then your challenge is to define and acquire these new skill sets. Today, many companies choose to outsource in order to gain access to these deep skill sets more rapidly.

Inaccuracy

Data quality is a notable problem in some organizations. Often, marketers believe they are thwarted by an absence of clean data. A company may find it has duplicate or redundant data. For example, databases could contain several different forms of someone's name (John Smith, J. Smith, John A Smith, JA Smith). Are these all the same person?

Unclean data can lead to the misclassification of customers, resulting in the distribution of unrelated offers, which can threaten the relationships you have been trying hard to cultivate and retain. Not only does poor data quality make data difficult to use, but also it adds a great deal of cost through unnecessary mailings and potential marketing communication corrections.

Also, organizations are reluctant to make decisions if they do not have faith in the data on hand. It is wise to avoid the potential for poor data to threaten the whole premise of Precision Marketing before it is launched. Marketers cannot be precise unless they carefully manage the resources that enable customer insight.

Inability to act

Organizations that have the access to their data and are able to precisely target key behaviours that benefit the company may have other limitations outside of the silo that will hinder Precision Marketing. These limitations include poor infrastructure, low-level expertise, lack of technology or a shortage of resources.

For example, we worked with a retailer whose objective was to increase online sales through e-mail and site visits. A logical approach would be to perform an analysis to determine the retailer's customers' propensity to purchase specific products and then to offer an associated cross-sell and up-sell. In this example we helped the retailer identify new distinct customer groups with different purchasing behaviours, along with some trigger marketing that could triple a customer's propensity to return to the site for additional purchases. In this case, although the insights were powerful and promising, the retailer was not able to deploy them because of a lack of resources, technology and processes in place to deliver the campaign.

Good practices at ING

ING Insurance is one company that has addressed the challenges of using customer data to get to know its customers in an impressive manner. ING built an enterprise information platform (EIP) that enables the firm to actively reuse data across different product lines and geographies. 'We've implemented repeatable processes,' explains David Gutierrez, Chief Information Officer for ING Insurance Americas. 'Our data model, our development processes, and our reporting are all reusable. That's been a big benefit.'[8]

How big a benefit is it for ING? The EIP, which enables the company to centralize data for easy distribution, has produced $450,000 in savings on each application requiring data profiles and $1.2 million in savings for each system requiring transaction details.[9] Not only has it enhanced data quality and provisioning, but also it has strengthened marketing programmes in nations throughout the world. This has helped the company transition from a product-driven to a customer-driven strategy. 'We're promising to treat our customers as individuals,' adds Gutierrez. 'Our main objective is to bring all our customer data together so that when you call us, we know you.'[10]

Other great sources of data

Savvy marketers look for data wherever they can find them. Often, third-party companies have useful data that they are willing to share or sell. There are multiple ways to gather data. Let's start with an example.

Leading Hotels of the World buys the data it needs

One company looking for more insight into its customers is Leading Hotels of the World (LHW). LHW is a small, exclusive organization representing some 500 independent luxury hotels, resorts and spas.

To expand its knowledge of existing and prospective customers, LHW went to American Express. 'The key here is the breadth and depth of the data available to us,' said David Bonalle, Vice President at American Express Business Insights. American Express has demographic, purchase and financial data on 54 million card holders.[11]

'Partnering with American Express can give us additional insights into customers we would normally know very little about,' said Claudia Kozma Kaplan, Senior Vice President of marketing and communications at Leading Hotels of the World. The result, said Kaplan, is that 'we can be much more intelligent about where we spend our resources with targeted, tactical offers, and we know for sure that we are advertising to a group of people that definitely are our clients'.[12] LHW set the objective to acquire new customers and opted to seek assistance from American Express to provide additional insights before deploying its campaigns.

'Analytics has been the hottest word [in marketing] for the past 18 months,' says David Frankland, Principal Analyst at Forrester Research. 'This trend is being driven in part by the economy, which has forced marketers to analyze their marketing spend more carefully to ensure profitability.'[13]

Touchpoint activity

Companies can work with third parties, as LHW did by partnering with American Express, to get external data. Alternatively, companies can use their own internal data, which are generated every time a customer interacts with the company. For example, every time customers buy something, they are saying, 'this fits my needs, lifestyle, and aspirations.' That represents pretty powerful data. If companies listen to the ring of the cash till and watch what each person buys, they can learn a tremendous amount about their customers. Loyalty programmes can markedly enhance data of this type by more firmly linking each purchase to a particular customer.

Collecting data on customers' activities, such as purchases and touchpoints, can generate staggering amounts of very individualized data, especially for repeat customers. No two customers are likely to buy identical products on identical days at identical locations. Touchpoint data can reveal:

- when customers bought;
- what they bought;
- where they bought it;
- how often they bought;
- what promotions they bought it with.

All these data provide insights into each customer's product preferences, consumption patterns and price sensitivity.

Many companies enjoy a direct source of this type of data. For example, retailers, travel companies, financial services, e-commerce sites and many B2B firms have direct connections with the end customer. These connections enable them to listen to each customer and know each customer by the customer's market basket contents. In other cases, such as consumer-packaged goods, a company sells in bulk to a distributor or retailer. These companies can obtain end-customer data from retailers or third-party vendors.

We have found that companies can increase their sales by going beyond demographics and sales data. Customers send a lot more messages to a company through a myriad of touchpoints, if only companies would learn to listen.

Jelly Belly's use of touchpoint data

For example, the Jelly Belly Candy Company sells a mouth-watering, mind-boggling range of jelly bean flavours. Customers can enjoy 50 full-time flavours and dozens of specialty flavours ranging from A&W Cream Soda to Juicy Pear to Sour Watermelon. For customers, finding flavours they like and avoiding flavours they don't like can be tricky. That hurdle leads to a lower response rate to Jelly Belly's e-mails and also causes some people to abandon their shopping carts.

To listen to its customers, Jelly Belly looked at:

- customer click-through data;
- search terms that customers used;
- site-navigation data;
- cart-abandonment activity;
- purchase history.

Each bit of data gives Jelly Belly some indication of what's turning the customer on, what's turning the customer off and what the customer is really looking for. Jelly Belly used this data both to improve the individualization of e-mail messages and to create a MyBuys intelligent product recommendation system. People who love flavours such as liquorice or buttered popcorn, for example, would see more of what they like in their e-mail alerts and web pages during search and navigation.[14]

Jelly Belly got sweet results from better use of the data. Specifically, it saw a 33 per cent lift in on-site conversions. In addition, 18 per cent of users acted on the personal product recommendations, and customers bought an average of 10 per cent more on each order.[15] The point is that even when a customer doesn't make a purchase, he or she sends other messages through other touchpoints. Companies can find a plethora of data through other, non-sales interactions with a company. These include:

- recorded voice interactions from contact centres;
- online product search and browsing behaviour;
- e-mail marketing activity (opens and click-throughs);
- customer service contacts (complaints, questions, repair/warranty activity);
- loyalty programme interactions, including usage patterns of loyalty rewards;
- requests for information;
- requests for coupons;
- comparison shopping views;
- view of branded content on social sites;
- pass-along rate of social offers;
- comments on blogs;
- sentiment analysis in support forums.[16]

New technology brings new sources of data

As marketers, we can imagine all manner of data that might be intensely useful to us. That's why we scan emerging new technology for new data-gathering opportunities and new ways to know the 'Me' of the customer. Every marketer has a wish list. At Polycom, a provider of communications technology to businesses, Chief Marketing Officer Heidi Melin says, '[T]he piece of data that would be most valuable to us that we don't currently have [involves] continuing to build intelligence around our customers, which products they have and how they're using them.'

These days, more and more products and services connect to the internet to upload or download data, update software, perform transactions or provide customer support. This means that, increasingly, companies can now gather data on what happens after the customer leaves the store or website. Companies can get a glimpse of how and when customers use their products. There's now even a WiFi-enabled bathroom scale that posts your weight to a secure website. We're not sure we want this for ourselves, but the product seems popular and we can see how it would be great for tracking New Year's resolutions or forming social support groups to help shed some pounds.

Best practices: reusing data, not re-asking for data

Regardless of how data are collected, one key is to use the data you already have rather than re-collect the data, especially if re-collecting data involves asking customers. If you have ever called a company's toll-free number and were asked by the automated phone system to punch in your account number and then transferred to an operator whose first question was 'What is your account number?', you know how frustrating and irritating it is for both you and the customer service representative to be duplicating the task.

Instead, the reuse of data extends to all levels of relevance marketing: reuse of data, reuse of insights, reuse of campaign results. Becoming truly relevant means using (and reusing) all that you can possibly know about the customer to understand what the customer wants and to communicate effectively with him or her. Collecting data is the second step to becoming a wiser precision marketer.

Collaborate to innovate

A Precision Marketing implementation entails close interaction between marketing and the predictive analytics team. After marketing objectives have been aligned with business objectives, the next step is to meet with all stakeholders to collaborate on data gathering. Consider including the analyst, the campaign manager, the IT Department, the agency of record and specialists to fully understand and document the goals of the projects and the timelines, schedules and available data.

Gathering data is a key step and necessary for success, but, as Chuck Martin once said, 'The result of bad communication is a disconnection between strategy and execution.' The Gather Data step is important because the analyst will rely on your insight to help create models to target specific behaviours. The analyst will need to understand and review the types of data you have on hand, so be prepared for a 'data discussion.' Be sure to ask questions on terminology if you are unclear, and provide clarification around your marketing terms, since all attendees will be using their own department's language and abbreviations. Finally, the analyst should make recommendations on specific sets of data that may need to be acquired from third parties or recommend new data that need to be identified.

Although the majority of modellers today use transactional data because they reflect customer behaviour directly, there are other data points that should be considered, such as:

- demographic data;
- purchased or third party data;
- campaign history;
- behavioural data;
- survey and poll data;
- contact history;
- GPS data;
- free-form data (social media).

Data are fundamentally important because data drive insight, insight drives relevance, and relevance drives customer loyalty.

> Data drive insight, insight drives relevance, and relevance drives customer loyalty.

The ongoing search for more data to create more relevance

Companies that do advanced analytics to improve precision and relevance are always looking for more data that might tell the company about customers. For example, the retailer Tesco has a marketing analytics subsidiary called Dunnhumby. Dunnhumby taps into both public and private databases to learn more about current Tesco customers as well as prospective customers. For example, Dunnhumby uses national data in the United Kingdom, such as the electoral roll, the Office for National Statistics and the Land Registry.[17] Dunnhumby also looks at private data sources such as credit reports to cross-correlate customers' spending patterns with financial variables.

Using search terms to understand customers

The words that consumers enter into e-commerce searches also provide an excellent indicator of what might be relevant to customers. For example, Tesco sells clothing at its large Tesco Extra stores, but only about half the UK population live near a Tesco Extra store. Using consumer search data led Tesco to create a dedicated online fashion store. 'Clothing is not only one of the fastest growing online markets, but the word "clothing" is also one of the most searched for categories at Tesco.com, so we know the site will be popular with both existing and new online customers,' said Terry Green, Chief Executive Officer of Clothing at Tesco.[18]

Demographics, psychographics and profiles

Since customers change their purchasing habits, addresses and employment, it is important always to have the most updated demographics, lists and profiles. Today's technology is able to take names and addresses and provide a multitude of information that will help the performance of your marketing efforts.

Given a name and address, companies can glean other data from a range of sources to identify the age, interests and psychographic variables of customers. Companies can gather some of these data from surveys or registration forms. If the company offers credit to customers, it can often gather credit information such as income and debt. Companies can use location data such as neighbourhood data that are tied to census blocks, postcodes or (in the United States) Metropolitan Statistical Areas (MSAs).

For B2B marketers, the analogue to a consumer's demographic data is a customer company's firmographic data. Firmographic data include variables such as headquarters or plant location(s), total employment, revenues and industry classification. Each firmographic variable lets the marketer craft precise content to suit the needs of companies in that situation. For instance, the size of the organization lets the marketer cite relevant phenomena that are common to firms of a given size, such as the need for multi-role managers in very small firms or regulatory issues that affect firms above a certain size. Another way to tailor the marketing message with firmographic data is to cite estimates of how much a company of that size might spend (or save) on certain products or services.

Industry classifications let marketers increase message precision with content such as key industry trends, recent industry news, common industry technologies, and references to key supplier companies or key customer companies with which the marketing target is likely to have a relationship. The point is that content customized for the customer's industry classification lets marketers show an understanding of the customer's key concerns or needs.

Mapping the customer: GPS and mobile data

By using location data, marketers can increase their precision in both picking the right people and picking the right messages for those people. Location data can be very powerful, and not just for demographic insights. Caeser's Entertainment Corporation (formerly known as Harrah's Casino), for example, computes the distance from its casinos to every customer it has in Caeser's loyalty programme. Why? Because Caeser's knows that for some local customers a trip to the casino can be a spur-of-the-moment fling; it doesn't have to be a long-pre-planned vacation. Therefore, locals provide Harrah's with a great opportunity for up-selling on frequency of visits.

As a result, Caeser's crafted promotional offers targeted specifically to locals. One of the offers, for example, gave locals free chips if they visited the casino in the next two weeks. The result of this promotion was impressive. After the promotion, locals went to their nearby Caeser's casino an average of 1.4 times a month compared to the previous average of 1.1 times per month – a 27 per cent increase in visitation frequency.

Location data can even be gathered online. Companies can deduce the location of online customers from the IP address of the customer's web requests. Even if the customer has not filled out a profile, the IP address data often pinpoint the postcode or MSA-level location of the customer. This information lets the marketer craft precise messages that might, for example, give the location of local retailers or reference some popular local phenomena (food, attraction, etc). The recent rise of device fingerprinting will help marketers piece together exactly who is on the other end of an internet cable. Fingerprinting companies such as BlueCava, Ringleader Digital and 41st Parameter get beyond the limitations of cookies to identify PCs and smartphones by their unique characteristics. Such data let the fingerprint company or its client company build profiles of the customer's activities, identify returning customers or associate customer activities across multiple channels. Reliably identifying people is the first step to engaging with people; if you don't know who someone is, how can you be relevant?

GPS is everywhere these days – in mobile phones, cars and stand-alone devices. These devices provide several services, from helping ease a tiresome commute to receiving instant coupons. Mobile devices in America are generating approximately 600 billion geospatially tagged transactions per day.[19] This new data source gives marketers another way to know where their customers are located. When you know your customer's location, you can provide location-aware services and marketing. In theory, companies could find out when customers pass by their store (but don't enter), or when customers enter the store (but don't buy).

In Australia, privately owned tollway companies leverage GPS information to improve the results of their marketing campaigns. For example, they will market their toll roads as a way to decrease commute time within specific traffic patterns while at the same time promoting discount coupons for the toll, which results in repeat customer business that drives traffic and tollway fees. GPS data are creating new businesses that make location awareness rewarding and part of a next-generation lifestyle. Start-ups such as Foursquare, BrightKite, Loopt and Gowalla let customers tag the places they visit, find nearby friends, post photos and instantly write reviews. Firms taking note of this powerful new insight are beginning to offer new incentives such as visitor loyalty rewards, advertising and coupons.

Quick polls and surveys

Today, it is very simple and inexpensive to conduct a quick poll on your website or blog, or via e-mails. These quick surveys provide a convenient opportunity to engage the customer, test an idea and provide that learning back to the marketing team. We recommend keeping these ad hoc surveys short – no more than three to seven questions – so that the customer can quickly answer them in a few seconds.

Surveys can ask a wide range of questions, such as:

- purchase/service satisfaction – 'How would you rate your recent purchase?';
- general attitudes – 'Would you recommend us to a friend?';
- product usage – 'When/where do you use your [company's product]?';
- competitor comparisons – 'Why did you buy our product instead of the competitor's?';
- messaging preferences – 'What features would you like to see in a monthly newsletter?';
- feedback on potential new products, new marketing campaigns, new web interfaces – 'If we offered you this, would you like it?';
- related lifestyle questions – 'How often do you use the product in the car/home/office?';
- defection or disengagement rationale – 'Why did you unsubscribe?'.

Short, sweet, and to the point: Verizon's one-question survey

We feel that even the simplest survey can be valuable. Posing a single question can reveal a lot about a customer and his or her feelings. We've noticed that Verizon includes a very simple one-question survey at the conclusion of many of its contacts with customers, whether online, on the phone or in person. Verizon simply asks, 'How likely is it that you would recommend Verizon Wireless to a friend or colleague?', with a 1–10 scale. Depending on the channel, there's also an opportunity for further feedback. If you're talking to a Verizon call centre and rate the company a big fat '0', the customer service rep will ask you why you feel that way. And if you answer positively with an enthusiastic comment, Verizon asks if it can quote you.

A number of companies now use this particular 'recommend-to-a-friend' question to understand the balance of people promoting or demoting their brand by using a metric and methodology called the Net Promotor Score.[20] The particulars of this metric are not the focus of this book and are not necessarily suited for all companies or all brands, but the larger point is the fact that simple questions can provide profound insights. All you have to do is ask.

In-depth, opt-in surveys

In-depth surveys are best when designed, conducted and fielded by an outside company that specializes in their design and delivery. While quick surveys get the pulse of the customer, in-depth surveys provide a much deeper well of knowledge. Sometimes a company would like to know a lot more about what customers think, how they use products, what else they do in their lives, what problems they face, how they see the future, and dozens of other details. Today, companies such as Survey Monkey and Zoomerang enable marketers to get information in days rather than the weeks it took previously. This new insight will need to be translated back to your analytic team, so be sure also to request the raw data and not just the summary of results. Even though only a small fraction of customers will participate in these longer surveys, the survey answers can provide a gold mine of information.

How Workforce Software uses surveys

B2B firms, in particular, use registration surveys to learn more about each customer's interests and needs. For example, Workforce Software, Inc. offered free premium content in exchange for more detailed registration information.[21] A relevant offer, such as a white paper, buying guide, webinar, trial software or product sample enables a company to ask more questions during registration. B2B registration questions might include the registrant's industry, job role, purchase intentions (eg 'immediate' vs. '6–12 months') and company size, all of which provide valuable data.

Workforce Software, for example, used the survey answers to compute a score for each registrant as a sales lead. High-score leads go directly to the company's sales force. Lower-scoring leads are handled by automated marketing processes.

Workforce Software also uses the registration survey data to individualize e-mails to each prospect. For example, the e-mail might say, 'I see you have a problem with union agreements' if that is what the registrant checked off.[22]

'I want to be able to quickly segment them and know who I'm talking to so that I don't go into my payroll manager speech when I'm talking to an executive,' says Bob Gallagher, Vice President of Marketing at Workforce Software.[23] The results? Using registration data to score leads helped Workforce Software handle a surge in traffic, and individualizing its e-mails to prospects improved the response rate.

Social media: customers' freedom of expression with free-form data

Social media are channels that not only let companies talk with customers but also give companies access to free-form customer data, which are also known as unconstrained written or spoken customer data. Most marketers today have allocated budget dollars to social media, but fewer have invested in the necessary technology to harvest the insights that can be gained from it. Data from social media channels are of value because the free-form data transcend the tick-box, multiple-choice, 1–5 ratings of most surveys and guided customer feedback. Free-form data let customers truly express themselves in their own words, which adds a richness and depth that lets companies know what customers really think.

How Gaylord Entertainment makes sense of free-form data

One company that is listening and responding to customers through free-form data is Gaylord Entertainment, an operator of convention hotels and entertainment venues such as the Grand Ole Opry in Nashville. The company sorts through all the raw data and aggregates them on approximately 300 types of customer issues.[24]

Yet Gaylord's experience highlights a common problem with free-form data. Converting raw free-form data into usable digital data took three to four weeks. While that time frame is fine for longer-term purposes, it is too lengthy for real-time correction of customer issues or marketing response to public relations problems. Moreover, Gaylord's original conversion process could classify only about 30 per cent of the raw data into more useful data. 'The other problem was that the old categories only showed us the quantity of a problem,' says Tony Bodoh, Manager of Operations Analysis for Gaylord Entertainment. 'We would be assuming that the quantity of data would be a proxy for the severity of a type of problem, which is often not the case.'[25]

Fortunately, software tools can now:

- rapidly process natural language;
- find key streams of thought;
- identify sentiment (positive or negative feelings);
- trace deepening chains of meaning within free-form data.

'By extracting concepts, names, sentiment, and other data from unstructured information, text analytics applications can give organizations a more complete view of their customers, leading to reduced customer churn, improved productivity and increased marketing campaign results,' says Susan Feldman, IDC's Vice President for Search and Discovery Technologies.[26] In Gaylord's case, the company used Clarabridge to automate the handling of listening post data. The processing times dropped to minutes and the depth and breadth of data conversion improved as well.[27]

As the Gaylord example shows, new tools can help companies really listen to customers. 'Internally focused voice-of-the-customer applications use sentiment analysis with transcribed call centre exchanges, providing insight into client issues on an individual or aggregate level,' says Nick Patience, Managing Analyst and Research Director of Information Management at The 451 Group.[28]

What relevance means for the business

If analytics is the engine under the hood, then data represent the fuel. Data tell companies about customers' salaries, residences, automobiles, leisure activities and purchase behaviour as well as many other variables. Every time a customer interacts with a company, the company has an opportunity to collect and learn from this data. Every time the company engages with a customer, the company should be thinking about how to listen and respond to that message. A company can be relevant only if it knows what customers want, and it can know what customers want only if it collects and analyses data.

Companies need to 'make sure they spend as much time thinking about the business decisions that should come out of CRM as they do about the communication and messages themselves,' according to Steve Goodroe, CEO of Dunnhumby USA.[29]

Step Two, Gather Data, is about embracing the value of customer data so that you can then leverage those data and other relevance-generating information for far more than just the optimization of marketing messages. Highly effective organizations integrate their data across functions and use customer data in all facets of the business, not just on marketing communication.[30] These effective companies move beyond silos or fiefdoms that don't coordinate between departments or business units.

Using 'We' to know 'Me'

The Gather Data step can be short or can it be long; it depends on the requirements. To a Precision Marketer, this step is necessary to validate that the right business objectives have been selected and to garner new insight, which will improve the analytic team's modelling efforts and improve your campaign results. Internal and external data give insights into the behaviour of our customers and social groups, and helps companies become relevant on a broader scale. Precision Marketers use this data on the 'We' to improve their marketing efforts to the 'Me'.

Precision Marketing means understanding your customer so you can help them to connect with your company. To do that, keep the following key questions in the back of your mind as you collect data:

- How can this piece of data improve our knowledge of this individual customer?

- How can this piece of data improve our knowledge of other existing or prospective customers?

- How would this piece of data enable us to be more relevant to the customer?

The next chapter continues the journey venturing from Step Two: Gather Data to Step Three: Analyse and Model. You'll discover ways to extract tremendous value from the data that you have gathered in Step Two. The rich customer insights that you need lie within the data and it takes deep expertise to create the analytical tools and models to extract and organize these insights to be actionable so that your strategy and tactics can deliver profitable results.

FIGURE 4.4 Precision Marketing Framework

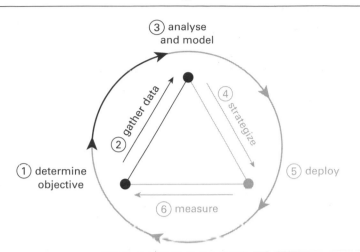

Key takeaway messages from Chapter 4,
'Step Two: Gather Data'

- Data are fundamentally important because data drive insight, insight drives relevance, and relevance drives customer loyalty.

- Extracting and utilizing data is challenging for the following reasons:
  - inaccessibility;
  - incomprehensibility;
  - inaccuracy;
  - inability to act.

- Today, there is no shortage of data. There are multiple sources available to buy, supplement and generate data:
  - transactional data;
  - demographic data;
  - purchased or third party data;
  - campaign history;
  - behavioural data;
  - survey and poll data;
  - contact history;
  - free-form data (gathered through social media or focus groups).

- Designing efficient data collection processes implies answering questions like:
  - What data can we collect?
  - Who can we collect data on (all customers or only some customers)?
  - How will we collect the data (point of sale, web, telephone, third party, etc)?
  - When will we collect the data (at purchase, quarterly, after a complaint, etc)?
  - Who will do the data collection (customer service representatives, specialized staff, third parties)?
  - Where will the data go (Customer Relationship Management, a special data warehouse)?

- If analytics is the engine under the hood, then data are the fuel.

- By using location data, marketers can increase their precision in both picking the right people and picking the right messages for those people.

- Even a single-question poll can reveal a lot about a customer and his or her feelings about a brand. Verizon's 'how likely is it that you would recommend Verizon Wireless to a friend or colleague?' question with a 10-point scale provides valuable information to the company. These quick surveys provide a convenient opportunity to engage the customer or test an idea.

- Social media give companies access to free-form customer data that are valuable because they transcend the constrained tick-box and multiple-choice formats of polls and surveys. Software tools can now be used to rapidly process natural language, find key streams of thought, and identify sentiment (positive or negative feelings).

Notes

1 CMO Council, Loyalty leaders: Feeling the love from the loyalty clubs, 2009.

2 Ibid.

3 CMO Council, Loyalty programs dole out rewards but fail to fully connect with consumers says new CMO Council study, 'Loyalty leaders: Feeling the love from the loyalty clubs', 2009.

4 Sharon Goldman, Triggers are in fashion, *Direct Marketing News*, 16 March 2009 [Online] **http://www.dmnews.com/ triggers-are-in-fashion/article/128773/**.

5 CMO Council, Loyalty programs dole out rewards but fail to fully connect with consumers says new CMO Council study, 'Loyalty leaders: Feeling the love from the loyalty clubs', 2009.

6 PricewaterhouseCoopers study 2004, cited by David Reed, *Precision Marketing*, May 2006 [Online] **http://www.qas.co.uk/company/useful-statistics.htm#=tab1).**

7 CMO Council, *Routes to Revenue*, 2008.

8 Jill Dyché and Evan Levy, Data integration success stories: ING Insurance Americas, in *Customer Data Integration: Reaching a single version of the truth*, John Wiley, New York, 2006, p. 179.

9 Ibid.

10 Ibid.

11 Chantal Todé, AmEx's new division displays value of data, *Direct Marketing News*, 14 December 2009 [Online] **http://www.dmnews.com/amexs-new-division-displays-value-of-data/article/159487/.**

12 Ibid.

13 Ibid.

14 Kimberly Smith, Case study: How a user-focused website boosted sales at jelly belly, MarketingProfs.com, 28 July 2009 [Online] **http://www.marketingprofs.com/casestudy/150.**

15 Ibid.

16 Forrester Research, *Customer Life-cycle Marketing Demands New Metrics*, 8 February 2011.

17 Heather Tomlinson and Rob Evans, Tesco stocks up on inside knowledge of shoppers' lives, *Guardian* (London), 20 September 2005 [Online] **http://www.guardian.co.uk/business/2005/sep/20/freedomofinformation.supermarkets.**

18 Sarah Clark, Tesco launches its online clothing store, *Internet Retailing*, 6 October 2009 [Online] **http://www.internetretailing.net/2009/10/tesco-launches-its-online-clothing-store/.**

19 Jeff Jonas, Your movements speak for themselves: Space-time travel data is analytic super-food!, 2009 [Online] **http://jeffjonas.typepad.com/jeff_jonas/2009/08/your-movements-speak-for-themselves-spacetime-travel-data-is-analytic-superfood.html.**

20 **http://www.cmo.com/taxonomy/term/922.**

21 **http://www.workforcesoftware.com.**

22 Ibid.

23 Amanda F. Batista, WorkForce Software sees 70% sales lift by automating marketing interactions, *DemandGen Reports*, 7 April 2009 [Online] **http://www.demandgenreport.com/home/archives/ demandgen-reports/195-workforce-software-sees-70-sales-lift-by-automating-marketing-interactions-.html**.

24 Jim Ericson, Service without reservation, *Information Management Special Reports*, 19 August 2008 [Online] **http://www.information-management.com/specialreports/2008_93/-10001822-1.html**.

25 Ibid.

26 George Makovitch, Organizations to understand and predict customer behavior with text analytics, *Information Management Special Reports*, 25 August 2009 [Online] **http://www.information-management.com/specialreports/2009_159/text_analytics_customer_behavior-10015951-1.html**.

27 Jim Ericson, Service without reservation, *Information Management Special Reports*, 19 August 2008 [Online] **http://www.information-management.com/specialreports/2008_93/-10001822-1.html**.

28 George Makovitch, Organizations to understand and predict customer behavior with text analytics, *Information Management Special Reports*, 25 August 2009 [Online] **http://www.information-management.com/specialreports/2009_159/text_analytics_customer_behavior-10015951-1.html**.

29 Devon Wylie, CRM case study 14, Tesco has links with the corner shops of England's past, 2005 [Online] **http://www.scribd.com/doc/43441362/Tesco-CRM-1**.

30 CMO Council, *Routes to Revenue*, 2008.

Step Three: Analyse and Model

> *The best parachute folders are those who jump themselves.*
>
> **ANONYMOUS**

In this chapter, you will learn:

- the four levels of the Segmentation Scale;
- the four descriptors of Precision Marketing messages;
- how to target the right person;
- how to choose the right channel;
- how to find the right time;
- how to create the right message.

Analytical models are creative, sophisticated tools that transform raw data into rich, actionable customer insights. It has been shown – clearly, quantifiably and extensively – that these insights provide positive outcomes. Because the data analytics and data models are critical to the precision and magnitude of the customer insights, it is important to utilize deep skills and expertise in Step Three. Let's start by looking at what a large hotel chain was able to do by developing and employing predictive analytical tools and models to mine an inactive customer base for high-value prospects.

Large hotel chain wakes up sleepy customers

FIGURE 5.1 Large Hotel Chain Overview

Large Hotel Chain	
Objective:	To re-engage dormant members
Strategy:	Create a high propensity model from existing members and apply the model to the dormant member database
Tactics:	To test dormant member engagement vs active member engagement in a summer promotion
Results:	1,090% ROI from the dormant member promotion

A large hotel chain's marketing department set itself the objective of re-engaging with the chain's inactive member base. The chain would leverage its existing data. The company faced the task of analysing and modelling those data to gain insights so that the chain could create targeted, relevant communications in place of its previous e-mail blasts. Although the earlier approach of sending out e-mail blasts was considered inexpensive, the company recognized that the risk of brand defection increases dramatically as a result of these irrelevant communications. Blast e-mails became ineffective as open rates plummeted. Liz Miller, the CMO Council's Vice President of Programs and Operations, says:

> It is no surprise that consumers are opting out of irrelevant emails. However, what is a grave sign for marketers to heed is that customers will disconnect and stop doing business with brands who continue to send messages that demonstrate a lack of intimacy, customer insight and individual understanding.[1]

The hotelier knew it needed a new approach to engaging with its members.

By following the Precision Marketing Framework, we and the Ricoh team helped the hotel chain find some hidden pockets of overlooked dormant members and helped deliver a good night's sleep to the large hotel chain. The objective was clear: re-engage dormant members (members who have not transacted in five quarters) to bring them back to the brand. Following the Framework, we scheduled a launch meeting for all stakeholders including marketing, IT, the ad agency and the print provider to discuss timelines, objectives, data requirements and necessary actions. The timelines were tight – a mere eight weeks – but all stakeholders were committed.

The Ricoh Data Analytics team was granted access to the hotelier's database, and the team began examining the data to learn how ideal, active members responded to current and past offers. The team cleansed and normalized the data and built an analytical model. These analytical models utilized five quarters of member transaction data to select inactive members with the highest propensity to re-engage with the hotel.

This high propensity segment, the 'sleeping beauties', had been dormant for more than a year, yet they received the same offer that the active members received. In the past, this 'inactive' segment would not have received any communications in order to save on the mail expense. However, analysis of the data revealed that the high-propensity dormant segment looked very similar to the high-propensity active segment, so we conducted a test. In the test we sent the same offer to active members as to inactive ones, given the similarity between these two segments. In less than eight weeks the hotelier saw an incremental revenue lift of 100 per cent relative to the company's existing marketing programme, and achieved a 1,090 per cent return on investment. In addition, the dormant test group outperformed the active group in all campaign metrics.

A 1,090 per cent ROI is an incredibly impressive result. More importantly, these results would not have been possible using traditional marketing business rules segmentation practices that do not leverage data, build analytical models and generate precise member targets. The point to underscore in the large hotel chain case is the fact that mining inactive data is a largely ignored but potentially rich way of generating incremental revenue. Reactivating dormant members is an approach that is much less costly than acquiring new members for incremental revenue opportunities.

The Segmentation Scale

FIGURE 5.2 Segmentation Matrix

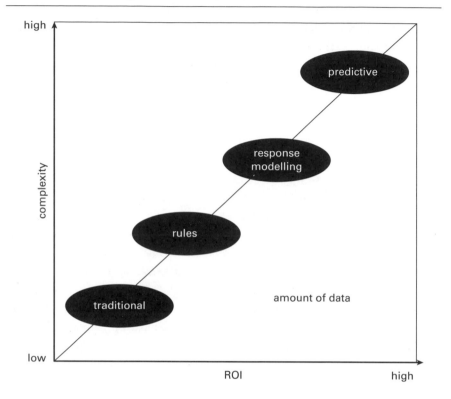

So how best to segment in a world that is mandating the requirement for relevancy to drive customer interaction? It seems just last year that many marketers were pleased with page hits and page views – but today the name of the game is getting your customer to interact with your products and services to build brand, revenue and customer loyalty. In short, the world is quickly moving from acquisition of new customers to proven or predicted outcomes with current customers to drive increased revenues.

How does your organization currently segment its customer base? We recommend using a scale to determine the level of segmentation complexity. The scale we use is a ranking that consists of four main segmentation techniques: *traditional*, *rules-based*, *response modelling* and *predictive*. In addition, we correlate the quantity of data leveraged in each technique to drive the best ROI. Companies can operate on any level of this scale depending on their business requirements, goals or challenges. For example, many credit card companies use predictive segmentation. It is in the nature of the credit card business that they collect vast amounts of transactional data, which can enhance the analytical modelling process. More data in this case equates with improved insight on consumer spending, payment patterns or even attrition. Meanwhile, a manufacturer that serves other businesses and makes complex products may have fewer data covering fewer customers. This company may choose to segment its customers using business rules or response modelling. Regardless of where you are on the continuum, your company can take steps to reach new levels of performance in analytical terms.

Let's take a more detailed look at the four levels articulated on the Segmentation Scale.

Traditional

Traditional customer segmentation is defined as the practice of dividing customers into groups of individuals with common characteristics. These segments help companies gain a better understanding of customers, then grouping them into categories to better optimize marketing programmes and resources spent. This traditional approach to segmentation can utilize many variables such as historical purchase data, gender, age and postcode. Many marketers leverage this insight by gathering data points such as the following:

- geographical areas such as regions, countries, states, postcodes, counties, etc;
- demographics: gender, age, income, education, etc;
- psychographics: lifestyle classification;
- sales channels, branches, and departments;
- product life cycle.

A good example would be a direct marketing mail campaign that targets women between the ages of 25 and 35 in postcodes associated with middle-class incomes for a specific offer. Analysis at this phase still remains relatively limited, but the very act of segmentation will provide a standard for comparison when the campaign is conducted. Reporting at this level tends to be historical in nature but will highlight the best-performing segments. Over time, the segmentation grows richer as marketers begin to rank customers by value, such as by segmenting customers into platinum, gold or silver categories.

Rules-based segmentation

Many marketers also define their customer segmentation according to behaviour, customer lifetime value and spend. This segmentation approach is focused on attracting and retaining the highest-value customers, which will drive a higher ROI and increased brand loyalty. Rules-based segmentation allows you to align messaging and offers a single variable (or set of variables) that is readily available in many databases.

This type of segmentation technique is frequently used in the retail, travel and hospitality industries. Predefined business rules determine the segmentation and award tier based on frequency and spend. Typically, the highest tier becomes some type of 'premium' category with the most perks, and those in that tier are then ranked accordingly on their perceived value segments. For example, in the large hotel group case study the marketing team used business rules to define its segments. Only customers who stayed within a specific time frame would receive direct communication from the hotel. The hotelier segmented its most valued guests as those who stayed most frequently, and this special segment would receive specific promotions.

Rules-based segmentation is quite a large spectrum. Best-in-class companies leverage their data to create robust segmentation and triggers. Others may be just starting and will use this type of segmentation to begin to collect data, behaviours and spend.

Whether you are a retailer promoting a fashion line or a travel company marketing a vacation package, you are making basic assumptions. If you have limited insight into your prospective customer's existing purchasing behaviour, then this is a perfectly appropriate place to start.

At the rules-based level, analysts use the bare minimum of data to find target customers. For business reasons, analysts may recommend relying on just one or few variables to determine a grouping. A simple example is making a special offer to prospects who did not already possess a credit card. The rule was: if the prospect does not own a card, make the offer. If the prospect owns the card, then do not make the offer. It's remarkable how much money could be saved – on direct mail alone – by rigorously following a simple, basic business rule of this kind.

CenterBeam's successful B2B segmentation campaign

CenterBeam is a B2B business that sells infrastructure management services. The company's objective was to gain more leads for the remote infrastructure managed services it sells to mid-market organizations. CenterBeam looked at organizations belonging to the top 10 best-performing SIC (Standard Industrial Classifications) codes and then drilled down to mid-market firms. In particular, it sought companies that were technologically compatible with CenterBeam's platform.

The company then pinpointed the chief financial officers (CFOs) within target firms and created precision message content for each vertical. Specifically, CenterBeam individualized the message by including recent news from the particular firm's industry. 'We're very particular about the target market and audience in that market and try to be pointed in the communications we deliver so that they are relevant to where they're going,' says Karen Hayward, Executive Vice-President and Chief Marketing Officer at CenterBeam.[2]

As the campaign progressed, CenterBeam updated content to stay timely, targeted and relevant. 'By focusing on high-performing SIC codes and delivering compelling outbound communications, we have been able to continue to generate high-quality CFO-level leads that result in orders in spite of an extremely difficult economy,' says Hayward.[3]

Response modelling

The first two approaches are based on historical insight, third-party information and a bit of art. Yet the CMO Council's 'routes to revenue' research highlighted that over 50 per cent of the marketers audited said they did not have good insights into retention rates, customer profitability and lifetime value of their customers, leaving half of the marketers targeting all customers segments regardless of whether they are high-value, low-value or no-value. This type of approach often results in a misallocation of the marketing budget, added noise and a minimal ROI. In fact, in the large hotel case study it was determined that the platinum segment did not generate the highest revenue.

The next approach begins to leverage collected data for segmentation. Response modelling identifies the similarities between responders from a marketing campaign and creates an analytical model that can be applied to new datasets to determine prospects that are likely to respond to a specific offer and those that are not.

The data are segmented by particular characteristics, historical responses or attributes. Customers who have engaged in a certain level of activity, for instance, might represent a 'high-value segment'. The challenge is to identify new or even inactive prospects that have similar characteristics and attributes. Response modelling is an important approach that analyses and examines the data to find 'look-alikes'. Once the data have been analysed and ranked, you can target the top responders and drop lower responders. Doing so will increase your conversions and reduce your marketing costs.

The large hotel group case study is a good example of a type of response modelling. The models were built to find inactive customers who shared many characteristics with the hotel chain's highest-value customers. The case study demonstrated that leveraging existing data is able to produce extremely impressive response rates. As companies move up the segmentation scale, it takes a higher level of analysis, resources and software to achieve this type of profile targeting.

Response modelling can be used to help companies prioritize and target marketing spend for customer reactivation, customer acquisition and cross-sell and up-sell possibilities to grow current customers as well as improve customer retention rates.

Predictive analytics

Wikipedia defines predictive analytics as

> an area of statistical analysis that deals with extracting information from data and using it to predict future trends and behavior patterns. The core of predictive analytics relies on capturing relationships between explanatory variables and the predicted variables from past occurrences, and exploiting it to predict future outcomes.

The simplest example to explain this concept is a person's credit score. Here, credit bureaus analyse past payment behaviours and current debt as well as other attributes and predict an individual's creditworthiness, resulting in a credit score. This type of scoring eliminates the need of the lender to 'go with the gut' to determine the amount of loan a person could repay and which interest rates to choose to factor in the risk associated with loan repayment.

This approach that credit bureaus take is very similar to what marketers can do. Predictive analytics extrapolates the information from the historical data, detects hidden patterns, compares the data and discoveries, and then determines likely future risk or business opportunities. No longer do marketers have to rely on the ad agency or their own intuition when creating, targeting and measuring marketing campaigns. The predictive analysis will model and score the best bets to achieve the company's objective. But this time it goes beyond response modelling. Here are some popular predictive analytics applications that marketers leverage to drive returns back to their business:

- cross-sell and up-sell offers;
- retention and attrition;
- product and portfolio mix.

Some marketers believe the ability to leverage data analytics is only in the domain of large companies, but today this is not so. Predictive analytics is now a critical skill for all marketing professionals as companies attempt to deal with increasing market pressures and economy. Precision Marketers who embrace data, analytics and campaign measurement will be well positioned to provide proven returns back to the business.

Predictive analytics moves beyond the reliance on historical events and predicts outcomes. The predictive models make it possible to gain insight on how customers will most likely respond to particular messages and offers, such as 'people who bought this title/book also bought these titles/books,' which increases revenue per transaction.

At this point, you are running Precision Marketing campaigns, appending the database with added variables, delivering relevant and personalized communications, and actively measuring your results. Through continual learning and refinement you develop a highly targeted marketing and messaging approach. Let's look at some examples of predictive analytics.

Example: Optus SingTel analyses social networks

One telecom company, Optus SingTel, used its calling data – 100 million calls a day – to map who knew whom and then to relate those data to customer behaviour. Optus proved what every marketer has always feared: when customers defect, they take their friends with them. Optus's data showed that when a customer leaves, the members of that customer's social group are four to five times more likely to leave as well. Fortunately, the flipside was also true. If Optus can attract a new customer, members of that customer's social group are four to five times more likely to join as well. The work doubled the accuracy of Optus's churn models, which predict churn in subsequent months using social groups, usage, billing, contract data and demographics.[4]

In another example, imagine an online retailer who recognizes that a particular beauty product has been purchased by a customer. Using predictive analytics, the retailer could leverage the data to generate the next best set of offers that the customer has a high propensity to purchase. It may be because other customers with similar tastes purchased the product. The purchased beauty product might be complemented by the new offer – or, alternatively, the online retailer might devise an offer to complement the purchased product with a related product, or send a new offer for a replacement that is timed to the prior purchase. In both cases the company is generating offers based on data that point to a future outcome.

Amazon is the classic example of using associative software to deliver extremely precise new marketing messages based on a customer's past purchases. When a customer buys books on a given topic from Amazon.com, Amazon will send alerts to him or her when new titles in that topic area appear. When a customer or prospective customer looks at a particular title, Amazon will show him or her 'people who bought this title also bought...', thus increasing the potential revenue per transaction through relevant up-selling. Amazon is continuing to evolve its use of historical data and using those data to customize messages that encourage additional purchases.

Wherever you begin on the Segmentation Scale, the key point is to get started, build momentum and develop new levels of capability. Your progression, however, depends on getting in the game in the first place.

Moving towards precision

For the purpose of relevance, Precision Marketing messages can be defined by four descriptors:

- the right person;
- the right channel;
- the right timing;
- the right message.

These are clearly interrelated: some channels support higher frequencies than do others; some types of rich content clearly belong in richer channels; and some types of quick content can come at higher frequencies. Analytics and modelling can help pick the right person, right channel and right time.

The right person

Finding the right person means finding the proverbial 1 per cent of people who will respond to your message while not sending the message to the 99 per cent who won't respond and will most likely dislike a spurious, irrelevant message. The right person depends strongly on your objective, which is one reason why defining the objective is such an important first step in Precision Marketing. For example, if retention is your objective, then the target is customers who are likely to defect. That means analysing customer profiles and behaviour for evidence that they are about to leave. Or if growth is your objective, then the target is current customers who do not buy all they could from you. That means looking at customer purchasing and demographics to see what the current customer might want but doesn't yet have.

Companies can make two kinds of mistakes in creating their targets for a marketing campaign. The first mistake is missing someone who belongs to the target group and who could have been engaged. These missed people are a lost opportunity and represent the potential upside in revenues from better data, analytics and modelling that do find all the right people. The second mistake is including the wrong people: people who are outside the target or who don't want to be engaged. These wrongly included people create added direct and indirect costs.

Traditional marketing focuses too much on finding as many people as possible without regard to their propensity to buy or their propensity to be angered by generic blasts of messaging. Generic broadcast blasts may not miss many people, but they create costs and collateral damage to the brand by imprecise inclusion of people outside the true target of the marketing effort. Precision Marketing, by contrast, focuses on finding the right people, and only the right people, for the campaign.

Companies are now taking a more precise approach that helps them reach the right people and hold the line on marketing costs. For example, StorQuest used Facebook ads to reach the right people. The company provides self-storage services in a number of college towns. Therefore, it wants to focus on people in that location who are attending those local colleges and who are likely to leave the college town for the summer. This goal meant targeting specific age segments among the student population. Older students, such as graduate students, are more likely to stay in town and thus could be excluded from the target. Facebook ads allowed StorQuest to reach the right ages and the right students at 21 colleges and boosted rentals by more than 50 per cent.[5]

The right channel

Marketers are seeing a growing array of channels from the recent explosion of smartphones, tablets and digital signage, and a growing variety of social media companies as platforms for customer engagement. Some traditional marketing channels such as newspapers, magazines and broadcast television may be declining in use. Others are changing. The advent of addressable ad systems on cable TV, internet protocol television (IPTV) and DVR systems converts the broadcast medium of television into a Precision Marketing medium.

The best channels for the right person, and right message

With these new channels come both the opportunity and the responsibility for making the right choice of channel. Picking the right channel means analysing and modelling the confluence of customers' channel preferences and the optimum medium for the message. Companies can analyse internal and external data on media consumption habits and response rates for their target population. In some cases, using a channel such as SMS or Twitter involves a two-stage process: marketing to get people to opt in and then judicious use of the channel for customer engagement.

Even the new media channels show differentiation of populations and applications. B2B marketers, for example, show stronger preferences for LinkedIn, Twitter and webinars when compared to B2C marketers. LinkedIn, for example, contains a much more professional demographic, making it a natural channel for reaching the right businessperson. Webinars provide B2B marketers with the opportunity to present a detailed rationale for products and information-heavy presentations about business-oriented products. In contrast, B2C marketers make more use of mobile and search engine marketing.[6]

More channels equals more integration

More than just shifting to these new channels, marketers must now support more channels simultaneously. Engaging the customer, especially for a loyalty programme, means letting the customer choose the channel. 'I think people are much more mobile now, in all the senses of the word. And you have to make the benefits of the reward program accessible on all channels. You need to allow the guest to decide how he wants to stay in touch,' says Barry Green, Head of Customer Relationship Management and Loyalty at Etihad Airways.[7] If the customer is always right, then the right channel is the customer's chosen channel.

Operating in multiple channels and picking the right channel means coordinating messaging across channels. A siloed approach, with different divisions handling marketing in different media, runs the risk of costly duplicate messaging, obfuscating the brand and missing the multichannel opportunities to engage customers. For example, Publishers Clearing House has long used direct mail marketing but then created a separate web effort. The disconnect meant the web team did not know who the loyal customers of the direct mail marketing side were and vice versa. 'We lacked cross-channel, customer-centric data visibility for our marketers, and the timeliness of the information we use to communicate with customers was too delayed,' says Rob Befumo, Director of E-mail Marketing.

To remedy the problem, the company started gathering data across channels and created a better system of warehousing data. 'Initially we had a database to identify potential win-back customers and target efforts appropriately, but going forward we'll begin reactivation programs earlier to prevent them from getting to that point.' With integrated access to data from all channels, Publishers Clearing House 'can identify lapses in customer engagement much quicker thanks to more accurate and efficient data systems,' Befumo says. The integration across channels created benefits. 'We've seen increases in sales revenue, new customer conversion, and payment on our "bill me" offers,' Befumo says.[8]

The right time

The right time means finding that window of opportunity between thought and action. The right time is before the customer takes action, such as purchasing your competitor's product. Yet a message shouldn't come too early because it needs to reach the customer when they're in a frame of mind to consider your message.

The question of the right time includes picking the right frequency (eg daily, weekly, monthly) and the right timing (time of day, day of week, etc). Analysis and modelling of responses, click-throughs and the like can help companies tune the timing. Some channels – such as SMS, online advertising and e-mail – provide fine-grain control over timing of the message delivery times. Although some channels, such as direct mail, cannot control when the customer sees the message, the flip side is that customers open the message at a time of their choosing. The customer chooses when to open direct mail or peruse a magazine.

Toyota Financial Services: a new lease on relevance

Choosing the right timing often means analysing events in the customer life-cycle to pick the right time and right message for those events. For example,

Toyota Financial Services set a goal to increase repurchases of leased cars. The company analysed customer repurchase behaviour to understand who repurchased, why, and when.[9] Toyota's data showed that a customer was especially likely to think about a car purchase as the end of the lease approached. A similar pattern occurred for car financing: people thought about buying a new car when their old car was fully paid for. This led Toyota to craft precision messages to different customer groups at different times, especially in the months shortly before the expiration of contracts.

The result? More precise messaging led to a doubling of the repurchase rate! And Toyota achieved this result while halving the volume of direct mailing. By predicting likely customer behaviour, Toyota could make timely and precise pitches to precisely selected customers rather than spraying all its customers with a generic pitch. Overall, the effectiveness of each message increased fourfold as a result of its relevance.

Time your message frequency to match customer activity

Although repetition seems to be a traditional marketer's mantra, it can be taken to dangerous extremes, especially with low-cost media that make high-frequency messaging possible. 'We've found that sending more messages doesn't mean better response. It's about the materials we're sending and their relevancy to the consumer,' said Tammy Lucas, Managing Director of Marketing Programmes at Best Western International.[10] In fact, excessive frequency kills engagements: 40 per cent of consumers cited 'e-mails are sent too often' as a reason for unsubscribing.

Royal Canin, for example, knows that customers do worry about marketing mayhem, so the company explicitly lists what and when messages will be arriving in the inbox when you sign up for PetFirst! membership. It typically sends e-mails about twice a month. Higher frequencies can work, but only if the messages match customer activity. For example, Tesco.com has an intensive e-mail messaging strategy but it times its message frequency to customer activity. Specifically, Tesco.com maintains a steady conversation with its 850,000 active online shoppers through:

- a generic monthly e-newsletter with online exclusive offers;
- an individualized bi-weekly alert;
- transaction-driven messages such as order confirmations and order satisfaction surveys.[11]

This more intensive message frequency befits both the low cost structure of e-mail and the direct relationship of customers with Tesco.com. Low-cost channels have the potential to support higher frequency, but only if customers find the higher frequency acceptable and relevant. Given that active users of Tesco.com order every three weeks or so, messages on a bi-weekly schedule are not excessive.

Seasonal messaging

Tesco.com also generates revenues from relevance through seasonal messaging. In 2006 a record-breaking 1.3 million shoppers chose Tesco.com to deliver their presents and groceries over Christmas.[12] 'Following the success of tactical digital activity booked around seasonal events such as Valentine's Day, we are ramping up our online campaign for Mother's Day flowers and extending it across all the portals to increase the reach,' says Andrew Barratt, head of online marketing at Tesco.com.[13]

An online marketing agency, Harvest Digital, planned and negotiated the media strategy. 'Although this is very much a direct response campaign we've discovered that with the right offer and the right creative we can make brand style placements work against strict CPA targets,' says Emma Wilson, director at Harvest Digital.

The right message

Creating the right message means knowing the customer deeply enough to tailor the message to be relevant to their needs. For example, pharmaceutical companies should engage in a conversation with consumers. Rather than just pushing a product, they can tailor their messages to address what patients are really trying to solve, such as a diagnosis or what medicines are right for them. As Becky Chidester, President of Wunderman World Health's Global Health Unit puts it:

> My experience has shown me how personal healthcare is to consumers. Despite the science (expressed in populations and cohorts), people still feel their medical experience is unique because it's based on their heritage, their lifestyle, and how they want to be treated. Patients interpret general information in terms of what is right for them, whether there are side effects or how other patients have been treated with medications. The ultimate need for consumers is to find the 'right solution for me,' and they will keep seeking information from others, expert or otherwise. The onus is on the healthcare community to continue to evolve.[14]

Chapter 6 will talk more about how to create the right message.

The predictive Precision Marketer

Some companies have discovered the power of predictive analytics to increase revenues, decrease costs and fine-tune business operations. However, many others wonder how to begin the journey. As you've seen, we began the journey together by Determining Objectives that aligned with business needs. We then moved to Gather Data to validate that objective. Now we will demonstrate how to begin using the data to generate insights in the next step in the Precision Marketing Framework, which is Step Three, Analyse and Model.

FIGURE 5.3 Precision Marketing Framework

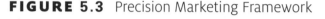

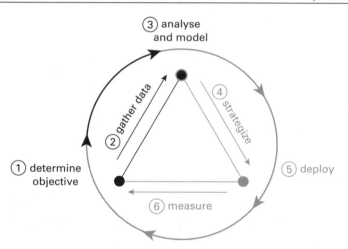

To begin this step, let's first review different approaches and definitions for analytics. It's easy to confuse terms such as 'descriptive analytics' or 'business intelligence' with 'predictive analytics'. Understanding the differences will assist in driving your success and achieving your objectives.

Descriptive analytics, also known as *business intelligence* (BI), is the most commonly used and widely understood term. It is a familiar term often incorporated into today's businesses operations. Descriptive analytics enables fact-based decisions, decisions founded on historical and/or real-time events.

Companies rely on the business intelligence team to generate reports in predefined structures and formats. These reports are used to explain how the business has performed to date. The information provided by the business intelligence team offers insights to operation managers and executives who base future business decisions on these insights. For example, a business intelligence report can provide historical insights on customer information, such as a particular income group, a specific geographic location, different sales levels or product purchases.

Business intelligence reports typically require some type of human interpretation to determine the next actionable decision. One limitation of this type of analysis is that these decisions may not always be the optimal choice for the business. BI reports are historical in nature. This implies they do not contain the information necessary to predict future events that can drive top-line results. For example, if a report was needed to understand a purchasing sequence in order to determine 'the next best consumer offer,' then this BI report can only report what the customer has done in the past, not what they might do in the future. These reports do not provide the information necessary to determine future behaviours.

Predictive analytics takes business intelligence to a more advanced level. It uses the information from the historical data, as does business intelligence. However, that is where the similarities end. Predictive analytics takes the information from the historical data, detects hidden patterns, compares the data and discoveries, and then determines likely future behaviours. This output, when interpreted properly and aligned with business objectives, can generate economic and organizational growth. With the benefit of predictive analytics, Precision Marketing can be executed with the right marketing strategy aligned to the right customer targets to deliver the most relevant product and/or service.

Business intelligence is an important resource, although it is not sufficient to take the business forward to more profitable strategies. Predictive analytics is the better choice to advance companies to new profit and performance levels. Predictive analytics can provide extraordinarily powerful insights which then enable marketers to consistently produce valuable results. Combining the power of Precision Marketing with the power of predictive analytics is how marketing organizations become the drivers of profitable growth and influencers of future corporate strategic direction.

FIGURE 5.4 Descriptive vs Predictive Analytics

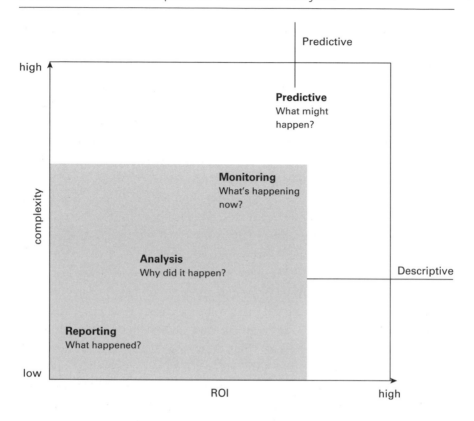

Hand over your data

Regardless of your company's size or market position, it is clear that you must dive into your data and begin cultivating insight if you are going to have a competitive advantage in the years to come. If you are to be truly relevant to your prospects and customers, you must actively mine your data to produce predictable, actionable insights. Data have now become the cornerstone of a Precision Marketer's success.

As was illustrated in the large hotel chain case study at the start of this chapter, we recommend holding a stakeholder meeting that includes representatives from groups such as marketing, data analytics, product specialist, IT and your creative agency or ad agency. The purpose of this meeting is for the marketer to provide data, perhaps on past campaign metrics, surveys, focus groups or quick polls. Then the IT department should deliver the necessary transaction data export. The next step is for the team to hand over the gathered data to the analytical gurus for them to apply their knowledge and skills.

The analyst must cleanse and transform the data, which is quite an arduous task but is imperative for improving marketing outcomes. The analyst will examine the data and perform a deep data cleanse. This step is necessary to remove the redundancies, errors and outliers as it normalizes the data into a readable format. After this process the file could be vastly larger as a result of all the insight that was collected in the Gather Data step and has now been cleansed and analysed.

Depending on skill sets, software tools, knowledge and resources, the analyst will review the data to determine the best targets for your specific business objectives.

Modelling for results

As in the large hotel chain example, a model might predict how to reach 70–80 per cent of the desired campaign results by targeting 30–40 per cent fewer carefully selected customers that have the highest propensity to respond and convert to a particular offer. Table 5.1 shows an example of how to optimize your marketing budget and achieve business results. In this example, rules-based segmentation is being compared to predictive analytics and modelling. The business rules state that any customer that has conducted business with the brand in the past 90 days will receive a promotion. The precision marketer is only sending promotions to customers that exhibit a high potential to re-engage with the brand (dormant or active). The result can be huge savings and far higher campaign ROI than you might achieve otherwise. What's more, the Precision Marketer can apply this perspective in many different contexts. Different models can be used to address different objectives.

The results are compelling. Whereas traditional marketing might enable marketers to produce more responses by reaching a larger number of customer targets, the key factors for Precision Marketers are response rates, profitable revenue and ROI.

By developing analytical models that target the right customers with a relevant message, Precision Marketers create campaigns that will produce far greater returns on investment. The concept here is that less is more,

TABLE 5.1   Modelling for results

	Traditional Marketing	Precision Marketing
number of customers targeted	20,000	2,000
cost per customer targeted	$5	$12.50
total communication costs	$100,000	$25,000
number of responses	474	222
revenue per responder	$210	$210
total revenue	$99,540	$46,620
response rate (%)	2.37%	11.10%
total profit	–$550	$21,620
return on investment	99%	186%

because less produces more. Each of the four primary marketing objectives (customer retention, customer growth, customer reactivation and customer acquisition) relies on the development of specific analytical models.

Customer acquisition

Customer acquisition remains a top priority for many marketers. Customer acquisition marketing is considered more costly than retention marketing. By leveraging predictive analytics, your campaigns can become much more targeted, which can greatly reduce your costs. The model provides a logical and cost-efficient way to target, communicate with and attract prospects that have the highest likelihood of responding and becoming a new customer.

Customer growth

Customer growth objectives rely on models that target customers to whom to cross-sell and up-sell. The goal is to leverage the model to make customers more valuable and profitable. Cross-selling has been a challenge for companies that offer multiple product lines. Targeting the right customer with the right offer can be a complicated process, but cross-selling of products leads to stronger customer relationships and loyalty. Predictive analytics helps get the right offer to the right consumer, at the right time. Insurance companies have long understood the benefits of effective cross-selling. In fact, insurance companies that can successfully cross-sell from an anchor product, such as car insurance, to home insurance have greatly decreased the odds of customer attrition. Supporting this point, the CMO Council's *What's Critical in the Insurance Vertical*[15] revealed that insurance marketers who currently offer product add-ons and/or cross-sell to their existing policyholders enjoy a 21 per cent conversion rate.

Customer retention

Increasing competition coupled with economic pressures is mandating that marketers improve their retention strategies. Research has proven that it is less expensive to keep a current customer than to acquire a new customer. When the focus is customer retention, predictive models may revolve around such matters as attrition risks, price sensitivity, spending habits or customer lifetime value. Retention modelling can help uncover existing customers with a high potential to be grown into higher levels of profitability.

Customer reactivation

Today, predictive analytics can model past customer churn and identify hidden trends and behaviours. Applying this new insight to your existing customer base will help highlight which of your customers are at risk of leaving the brand. This gives you an early warning indicator to proactively establish plans to prevent the defection. Banks frequently use this approach to detect when a high-wealth customer begins to move his or her funds to another bank. This detection allows the bank to make personal calls and offers that will help prevent the customer from leaving and taking their money to another banking institution.

In addition, models can focus on the recovery or reactivate customers who are currently disengaged or who have a deteriorating relationship with the company. This type of modelling may measure win-back propensity or unrealized value potential by predicting the next best action that could win the customer back.

Vertical pain points and risks

Predictive analytics can be used in many ways to help avoid risks, streamline operations and provide new opportunities. Today, many companies are using predictive modelling to help deter fraud and optimize city infrastructures, and in criminal profiling. Analytics can also target potential slow payers, and enable you to know which payers can directly affect your bottom-line results. The key to success remains in the data, assumptions that are created and the testing of the model.

Finally, at the end of the analysis, recommendations are delivered back to the team. The analyst will deliver new insights that help formulate the right strategy. New targeted customer sets may have been revealed, as in the case of the large hotel chain, that optimize marketing spend as well as deliver strong results for the company. Without such actionable insight, marketers fly blind or partially blind, using their traditional segmentation models rather than targeting the behaviours that are determined by predictive analytics teams.

In the journey from Determine Your Objective to Gather Data and now to Analyse and Model, you have completed much of the groundwork that will allow you to strategically determine the next best actions for your campaign. The data have been gathered, architected and analysed. This new insight, the analytical recommendation, will now drive the strategies and campaigns that are aligned with your business objectives. Whether marketers are focused on objectives such as acquiring, retaining, growing or winning back customers, the analytical model will help target the individuals who are most likely to respond to a particular campaign, promotion and/or product.

The findings produced in this analytical investigation will have a stronger impact on the messages that will resonate with the target audiences, the most effective channels and other factors that will contribute to downstream success. Although analytical investigations cannot fully predict outcomes, they can provide the backbone to form solid hypotheses that can be rigorously tested and validated.

Grounded insights with disciplined analysis are the forces that will separate campaigns from the costly and disappointing to the revenue-producing and positive ROI-generating. As other marketers cling to old habits, namely experience and intuition, the Precision Marketer can rely on predictive analytical approaches that leverage data and deliver relevance. This insight will help Precision Marketers outperform their peers in the years to come. As we'll explore in the next chapter, the move from Step Three, Analyse and Model, to Step Four, Strategize, is where Precision Marketing really gets real.

FIGURE 5.5 Precision Marketing Framework

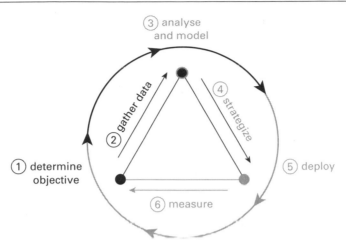

Key takeaway messages from Chapter 5,
'Step Three: Analyse and Model'

- Data analytics and the creation of data models are key components that drive the actionable insights for Precision Marketing.

- Deep and specialized skills and expertise are required to develop and employ data models and analytics on an ongoing basis.

- Most companies use analytics today. Analytics can be described on a continuum that increases ROI exponentially as other inputs increase, such as amount of data, levels of sophistication and complexity. The four steps on the Segmentation Scale are:
  - traditional;
  - rules-based segmentation;
  - response modelling;
  - predictive analytics.

- Many companies utilize rules-based segmentation and think that their actions are data analytics. Although this is true, rules-based segmentation is not an optimal level of analytics to employ. Moving to predictive analytics modelling will require investing more in data, sophistication and complexity but in return the company will gain increasingly better returns. The bottom line is that the returns are worth it because ROI can increase at a much greater rate than the input areas.

- Data analytics and models can help companies with four growth initiatives:
  - customer retention;
  - customer growth;
  - customer reactivation;
  - customer acquisition.

- Analytics matter. The purpose of analytics is to convert and translate data into actionable, profitable customer insights.

- Targeting the right person requires analysing customer profiles and behaviour, focusing on precision, not quantity.

- Choosing the right channel means analysing and modelling the confluence of customers' channel preferences and the optimum medium for the message.

- Companies can analyse internal and external data on media consumption habits and response rates for their target population.

- Finding the right time means timing the message before the customer has purchased but not so early that they're not in a frame of mind to consider it. Finding the right time also includes picking the right frequency (eg daily, weekly, monthly) and the right timing (time of day, day of week, etc). Analysis and modelling of responses, click-throughs and the like can help companies tune the timing. Some channels – such as SMS, online advertising, and e-mail – provide fine-grain control over timing of the message delivery times. Although some channels, such as direct mail, cannot control when the customer sees the message, the flip side is that customers open the message at a time of their choosing. The customer chooses when to open direct mail or peruse a magazine.

- Creating the right message means knowing the customer deeply enough to tailor the message to be relevant to their needs.

Notes

1 CMO Council, *Why Relevance Drives Response and Relationships: Using the power of precision marketing to better engage customers*, 17 November 2009.

2 Kimberly Smith, Case study: How a targeted lead-development program earned an IT company 34% yearly growth for five years (and counting), MarketingProfs.com, 27 January 2009.

3 Ibid.

4 James Taylor, Know your customers by knowing who they know, 20 October 2009 [Online] **http://jtonedm.com/2009/10/20/ know-your-customers-by-knowing-who-they-know-paw**.

5 How 12 companies are leveraging the social network to advance their marketing objectives [Online] **http://nadinefisher.com/facebook/Facebook.pdf**.

6 Social media hits mainstream; tried-and-true still works best, 11 August 2009 [Online] **http://www.marketingcharts.com/interactive/new-media-hits-mainstream-tried-and-true-still-works-best-10087**.

7 CMO Council, Gauge the love in your loyalty club [Online] **http://www.loyaltyleaders.org/expert-insights.php**.

8 Jeremy Nedelka, From data to dollar$, *1to1 Magazine*, 23 February 2009 [Online] **http://www.1to1media.com/view.aspx?DocID=31426**.

9 Graham Hill, It's time for a balanced scorecard for customer data, CustomerThink, 15 March 2009 [Online] **http://www.customerthink.com/ blog/it_s_time_for_a_balanced_scorecard_for_customer_data**.

10 Thomas Haire, Best Western melds old and new, *Response Magazine*, 1 March 2009 [Online] **http://www.responsemagazine.com/ response-magazine/best-western-melds-old-and-new-1346?page_id=2**.

11 Dave Chaffey, Tesco case study and Tesco.com case study for e-commerce and internet marketing [Online] **http://www.davechaffey.com/ E-commerce-Internet-marketing-case-studies/Tesco.com-case-study**.

12 Sales frenzy as retailers offer huge discounts, *Mail Online*, 26 December 2006 [Online] **http://www.dailymail.co.uk/news/article-424802/ Sales-frenzy-retailers-offer-huge-discounts.html**.

13 Tesco runs online advertising campaign for Mother's Day, Harvest Digital, 7 March 2007 [Online] **http://www.harvestdigital.com/news/article/ tesco-runs-online-advertising-campaign-for-mother-s-day**.

14 Ira J. Haimowitz, *Healthcare Relationship Marketing: Strategy, design and measurement*, Gower Publishing, Farnham, 2011.

15 CMP Council, What's critical in the vertical – insurance, 2010.

Step Four: Strategize

> *Knowing is not enough; we must apply.*
> *Willing is not enough, we must do.*
>
> **JOHANN WOLFGANG VON GOETHE**

In this chapter, you will learn:

- how to create your customer strategy;

- how to use the Communication Matrix;

- how to create relevant content and develop the right message;

- how to craft measurable content.

In Step Four, Strategize, your task as a Precision Marketer is to outline a specific, actionable plan to achieve the objective based on the customer insights gleaned from the data analysis. With Step Three complete, the research has been done, the insights generated and the opportunities identified. Now comes the time for applying those insights to design and outline a real market activity. Thus, the strategy or plan is ready to be developed and articulated so that action and traction can occur. ING Bank is a great example of developing and aligning a strategy for action, so we start this chapter by discussing the Precision Marketing approach taken by ING Bank.

FIGURE 6.1 ING Bank Overview

ING Bank	
Objective:	Increase productivity of direct marketing efforts through relevance
Strategy:	Implement an enterprise-wide campaign management system to support business analytics and multichannel campaigns
Tactics:	Set up a customer contact team, utilize business analytics and employ new monitoring and metrics
Results:	Response rates for savings accounts rose as high as 60%; direct marketing costs projected to fall 35% per year; campaign cycle times have improved, dropping from 26 weeks to 4 weeks

As we consider the case of the Netherlands-based ING Bank, we see the importance of its methods to create its tactics. Confronted with diminishing productivity in its own direct marketing efforts, the bank successfully transformed its marketing approach to focus on multichannel interactions. The strategy ING developed brought a transformation that enabled the bank to become far more relevant to its customers. ING determined its objective in order to create its strategy. 'By implementing a centralized campaign management program that creates personalized offers in real time and can deliver them through multiple channels, ING has increased average campaign response rates and expects to reduce its direct marketing costs by 35% per year,' states Alexander Hesse, an analyst with Forrester Research, in a recent profile of the company.[1]

The bank had become dependent on direct mail as its primary marketing vehicle. As one of the largest financial services firms in Europe, ING was producing 60 million direct mail pieces annually.[2] However, it was failing to reach its customers in a relevant fashion. While it communicated with them through direct mail, e-mail, websites and call centres, the varying channels lacked integration. In addition, each separate division within ING employed its own contact and communication approaches.

Moreover, the bank was slow to execute. Outbound mail campaigns often took between 16 and 22 weeks to design and launch. It would then take another 6 to 8 weeks to measure the campaign's impact and produce clear results. Together, each campaign took anywhere from 22 to 30 weeks from implementation to measurement – a total of over six months. Such long time frames made it difficult to refine campaigns and produce enhanced outcomes.

Considering that the bank was running 650 campaigns per year, its skill in direct marketing was strong. However, response rates were dropping steeply. Between 2005 and 2007, campaign profitability fell by as much as 65 per cent on average[3] (Figure 6.2).

FIGURE 6.2 ING Bank's Campaign Metrics

Campaigns per year	Average total campaign time	Campaign profitability
650	4 weeks	−65%

ING realized its marketing messages were lacking relevance. Why? Minimal customization was one key issue. Marketers were relying on generalized business rules to guide their efforts. Product-driven campaigns were produced that led to all prospects receiving the same offer. One large campaign for mortgage loans delivered conversion rates of just 0.08 per cent.[4]

ING marketers also realized they were failing to engage in an ongoing dialogue. While the direct mail engine for producing outbound campaigns was in full gear, there was little effort to deliver subsequent messages based on a prospect's initial response. Nor was there much investment made to engage customers in a personal way through inbound channels such as on-line banking, contact centres and retail branches.

Recognizing the need to rethink its marketing strategy, ING embarked on a 15-month project involving 50 employees from marketing, IT and the company's varying channels. The project involved implementing an enterprise-wide campaign management solution that could effectively employ analytics and business rules to support multichannel campaigns. One of the key factors that the new solution allowed was the ability to generate 'next best actions' in real time, enabling marketing to make relevant offers in various channels.

To accelerate marketing decisions, ING also set up a dedicated customer intelligence team responsible for executing all campaigns and a 'customer contact direct team' to coordinate with the various channels. Finally, the project team introduced new monitoring and measurement tools to report on campaign response rates, net present value and revenue. The dashboard gave marketing decision makers a comprehensive view of sales funnel progress and campaign results.

As a result of these efforts, efforts that mirror the Precision Marketing Framework, ING's marketing organization is now able to generate relevant marketing messages through various channels on a real-time basis. This means ING can support customer engagement in both inbound (branches, contact centre, the web) and outbound (direct mail, e-mail, outbound calls) channels. It also can synchronize its messages across these channels, ensuring that customers receive messages that are consistent. Indeed, the bank can now create relevant messages on many levels. This ensures that marketing takes the next best action that is appropriate on the basis of each customer's profile, behaviour and past interactions.

FIGURE 6.3 ING Bank's Improved Campaign Metrics After Analytics Employed

Campaigns per year	Average total campaign time	Campaign profitability
650	4 weeks	+65%

When ING measured the results of its new Precision Marketing-based efforts, it found strong results. Campaign response rates for savings accounts rose as high as 60 per cent[5] (Figure 6.3). And, as mentioned, direct marketing costs are projected to fall 35 per cent per year owing to increased efficiencies and automation. Finally, campaign cycle times have improved, dropping from 26 weeks to 4 weeks. This enables ING marketers to refine their campaign approaches more rapidly, incorporating lessons learned into each new campaign. Clearly, ING has proved quite capable of executing a Precision Marketing strategy to produce powerful outcomes.[6]

The strategy phase

ING, like many companies today, was faced with declining response rates owing to irrelevant content and offers, as well as strategies that were misaligned with business results. Fortunately, ING demonstrated the foresight to recognize this opportunity and address the inefficiencies by implementing a data-driven communication strategy for marketing campaigns. As the ING case vividly demonstrates, the recognition and implementation of key Precision Marketing strategies and tactics, combined with the alignment of actionable insights provided by the analysis, can produce relevant messages that drive a positive impact to the top line.

The strategy phase helps to ensure that marketers do not fall into the trap of marketing to the wrong target set of customers. If a company markets to the wrong target segments, it adds to the irrelevance and further increases brand defection, not to mention the misallocation of budget which will not provide a return back to the company. Typically, the analytic team will deliver recommendations based on the goals, business issues or opportunities that were outlined together with the marketing team. The strategy phase takes the data that were mined, analysed and modelled by the analytical team and makes those insights actionable. The analytic team used the data to identify potential new customer segments and their propensity to respond. For example, a ranking could generate a new target audience, reveal specific price sensitivity, or point to an under-marketed city or region. As a result, these new insights, rankings and recommendations will shape an effective strategy for a new campaign.

Creating your customer strategy

Performing rigorous analytics and modelling is necessary for strategic decision making. Data do not lie. 'Tried-and-true' gut decisions may mislead and misdirect strategic actions and funds. The analytical team's analysis consists of interpreting hundreds of thousands to millions of records and should reveal new insight into achieving new goals, finding opportunities or solving business problems. Through data-driven insight, a company can achieve a deeper understanding of a customer's actual value and propensities to purchase. This, in turn, drives the strategy and determines the campaign, deliver channels, tactics and offers.

You can now:

- confidently decide which newly defined segments to target;

- delineate what offers the new segments will have the propensity to purchase;

- match what message, in what channel will resonate with your target segment(s);

- determine the best channel to drive your strategy, eg direct marketing, e-mail, banner ads, telemarketing or some combination;

- decide whether a new campaign will be needed, or create a new one;

- outline what content and creative to incorporate into the campaign;

- plot and confirm the metrics for success, conversion rates and how to measure the results;

- determine which prospects receive which promotion.

These are just a sample of the types of strategic objectives you can have in creating your strategy. The more metrics you define, the better your ability to adjust the campaign. Remember, clearly outlining and defining these questions enables you to create the strategic and supporting tactical actions required to achieve the outlined objectives. The predictive analysis helps answer these questions to determine which prospects to target, the preferred channel mix to use, and which offers to best engage customers. To further clarify the power of analytics, Figure 6.4 is an illustration of a sample quadrant that demonstrates the information you can garner by rankings on new segments or 'best bets' to achieve the desired outcome.

FIGURE 6.4 Response and conversion matrix

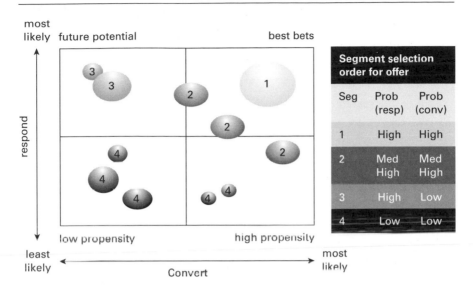

This illustration is a sample ranking system of customers used in the hotel industry. The analysis has broken out the new segments and placed responders into four quadrants on the basis of their propensity to respond to a specific travel offer. As you can see, the quadrant recognizes two key axes: current revenue and potential revenue. It then allocates responders into four categories: low propensity, future potential, high propensity and best bets. To which quadrant would you want to direct your campaign?

- *Low propensity.* This grouping refers to prospects or customers who represent both low existing revenue and low potential. In the example here, this segment has the lowest chance of re-engaging with the hotel chain, or may be a new customer. Sending expensive direct mail at this time may not be the best use of funds. E-mails and surveys may be the best channel through which to leverage this group.

- *Future potential.* This grouping refers to customers who represent high existing revenue but low potential revenue. This segment currently generates revenue for the company but does not have a high propensity to generate significant revenue in the future. In this example, targeting the occasional user does not represent the best allocation of marketing budget dollars to maximize incremental revenue back to the hotel chain.

- *High propensity*. This grouping refers to prospects or customers who represent low existing revenue but high potential revenue. Here, the 'high propensity' segment has greater potential than the other two quadrants, yet the strategy needs to consider a less costly form of communication to re-engage and grow this segment.

- *Best bets*. This grouping refers to customers who represent high existing revenue and high potential revenue, clearly the most attractive group. We refer to customers that represent the highest levels of existing and potential revenue as the 'best bets.' This was the group selected in the large hotel group example.

In the large hotel group case study detailed in Chapter 5, the analytics found a profitable customer group that was overlooked and therefore undervalued and under-leveraged by conventional segmentation and business rules. By following the Precision Marketing Framework, new insight revealed an untapped – and rich in potential – customer segment for which a customized strategy was formulated to achieve incremental revenue results immediately upon campaign deployment. Surprisingly, it was determined that the most engaged segments did not fall within the company's traditional 'platinum' segment.

The strategy phase revolves around rethinking the key elements of your existing marketing mix – in terms of your customers' interests, purchasing propensities and behaviours, which have been unveiled through analysis. Now the information must be transformed into actionable insight and aligned with your business objectives to drive measured results for your company.

Next, we will go to the Communication Matrix, where you chalk out specific strategies to build on what you have discovered in your analysis stage. You will now develop your plan on the basis of the data-driven insight that the analysis uncovered.

The Communication Matrix

The Communication Matrix is a tool we use in conducting workshops with our customers. It's a simple template but it charts out what channel, message or offer goes to which segment. It can be used for a new campaign or to understand an old campaign.

FIGURE 6.5 Marketing Communication Matrix

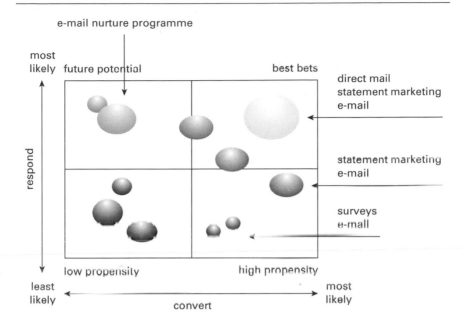

As simple as it seems, it is crucial to ensure that multiple departments are not all sending offers to the same individual. Unfortunately, this happens too often; all of us receive several offers in one week from a single company. According to research, *Why Relevance Drives Response and Relationships*,[7] 75 per cent of people polled said they received promotions for products that they had already purchased. In a workshop with a large bank in Asia, we determined that over 1,080 requests for names out of the CRM database were requested by 10 different product departments within six months. While the campaign management tool did have business rules in place, they were siloed by department and product. The software monitored the communications for each product line to allow the delivery of no more than two e-mails per month per banking product to the same person; however, it did not prevent a potential customer from receiving over ten product offers in one day! This type of error can be easily avoided by using the communication matrix.

The communication matrix helps avoid over-communicating and redundancy, which can be a costly error both from a financial and from a customer relations standpoint. By mapping particular messages to specific targeted segments, you can use the Communication Matrix as a tool to organize a prescriptive and customer-centric approach across all product lines.

At this point, you are well prepared to create your strategy. You are armed with new insights into your target customer, and you have defined the offer and the channel. Next, you will have to create, design and deliver with your creative teams.

Strategy in action

Today, the Precision Marketer is tasked with the responsibility of integrating the agency's creative with defined business objectives and voice of the customer. Once the target segment has been identified, and the high-level Communication Matrix has been completed, you must now brief your creative partners – both internal and external – on your new insight.

The Precision Marketing Framework requires the creative team to engage early in the strategy process. Bringing in the agency or creative talent to meet with the analytics team to discuss predictive analytical findings provides an opportunity for the team to gain a deep understanding of customer preferences. This meeting allows both teams to work together to translate the insights from analytics and segmentation into meaningful creative and content. Creative imagery and copy may now be fine-tuned and aligned to the new segments that were detected and, most important, to the preferences of the customers in those segments.

Precision messaging development is a strategy for better content across all channels and frequencies. Generic messages are irrelevant regardless of how often they are repeated or by which means they are sent to the customer. That observation complements findings from the CMO Council in its annual 'Routes to Revenue'[8] international audit of 650 senior marketers. The CMO Council study found that making communications more personal and relevant was among the top strategies for realizing greater revenue and profitability from existing customers. And content is clearly one of the most direct paths to relevance. *Better* content is clearly one of the most direct paths to relevance. Today, business marketers spend an average of 30 per cent of their marketing budgets on the creation and execution of content, according to a study conducted by Junta42 in conjunction with *BtoB Magazine*. 'That number could increase to 50 percent very soon, as the economic climate is triggering marketers to pay attention to the use of strategic content even more,' notes Joe Pulizzi, Junta42 founder and Chief Content Officer.[9] Junta42's research indicates that 56 per cent of marketers increased their content marketing spending in 2009, and just 4 per cent decreased their spending. 'Content is now the engine that makes marketing go,' Pulizzi says.[10]

Collaborating with your creative partners

Although very much in use today, the 1990s advertising agency approach can be problematic in this era of marketing-rich, relevant content and measurability. In the past, marketing and advertising agencies majored on slick creative to drive awareness and demand to a brand. Today, a majority of the public are no longer attracted to outlandish advertising practices. Products are expected to differentiate the brand (think Apple). Today's consumer is savvy in leveraging the internet, consumer reviews and social media before making a significant purchasing decision.

As a result, the relationship with agencies and other creative partners is dramatically changing. Going forward, Precision Marketers will work much more collaboratively with their creative partners and will be expected to share the insights delivered from analysis, new target segments, channel preference and propensities. The agency will play a critical role in interpreting the factual analytical findings and translate this insight into creative efforts that will further support the strategic goals. The facts and analysis change the dynamic. No longer do ad agencies have to rely on a marketer's gut feel for creative direction; agencies are now empowered to create based on data-driven insights, enabling the creative agency to become an extension of the Precision Marketer's practice. Now, the agency's work becomes data driven.

Developing relevant content

It is not uncommon to put the creative sizzle before the customer's needs. Think about those television commercials that seem to be too loud and seem to beg for an order by saying, 'But wait! If you order now...' In other words, not only has creative been left to the agencies' expertise or in-house talent, but content has been left behind, too. Many times neither the agency nor the in-house talent has access to the insights that have been uncovered in the Precision Marketing Framework to fine-tune their creative content.

As marketers ourselves, and from our work advising clients, we have established the practice of heavily scrutinizing ad copy and imagery to make sure it is relevant to our buyers. At times, we are puzzled by what we share with the ad agency and how that information is interpreted and prototyped. Since we are in a B2B company, our customers are purchasing $2-million-dollar products, which means our customers want less fluff and puff and more relevant content, customer advocacy and analyst reviews. Somehow, in one of our past campaigns this got translated into a sizzle campaign that involved a swimmer. We can tell you that our target market is aging and could rarely connect with a youthful young man with a skateboard that included some irrelevant copy. Frankly, we were speechless. Back to the drawing board, with a delay of another six weeks.

We have all experienced this from small to the largest agencies. Marketers will spend days updating the agency, internal teams, editing the points of view and then finally, after weeks of work, the agency reveals its creation. Sometimes it is right on, and other times it is... a complete miss.

Since the Analyse phase is the backbone to the Strategy step, using this insight can greatly reduce misinterpretation and helps to maximize a marketer's efforts in the shortest amount of time. New trends, traits, segments, behaviours that may have gone unnoticed are now revealed. Today the agency receives a very clear, data-driven perspective on the newly defined targeted customers. This allows for much more targeted copy that resonates and moves the buyer to a predetermined outcome.

Developing content by using focus groups

The Los Angeles Department of Water and Power (LADWP) focuses on focus groups

FIGURE 6.6 LADWP Overview

Los Angeles Department of Water and Power (LADWP)	
Objective:	**Primary:** To be the greenest city in the United States
	Secondary: To meet the state-mandated carbon emission regulation
	Third: To reduce customer call centre inquiries by 20%
Strategy:	Make the billing statement a clearer and more compelling customer communication vehicle that would drive green behaviours
Tactics:	Conduct focus groups to guide the statement redesign priorities
Results:	Underway

Another method to create customer-centric content is to gather customer feedback through focus groups. Focus groups are still a popular way to solicit feedback from a representative sample of your target customer segment(s). They have provided insight for decades and can continue to be leveraged for testing strategies and tactics prior to deployment. Given the cost of potential campaigns, new branding efforts and corporate mergers, focus groups represent a wise investment.

While focus groups have been used for decades, the Precision Marketer uses them in a slightly different way. Analogous to the way that Hollywood tests its films for success or failure with studios on standby to rework and reshoot film segments on the basis of feedback, so the Precision Marketer needs to be agile in order to react to real-time customer insights.

Utility companies have been known for sending statements that look plain and are often confusing, as seen in Figure 6.7, for example.

In an industry without competition, customer communication was often an afterthought. With the advent of smart meters, which allow utilities not only to monitor consumption more accurately but also bracket that consumption into accelerated fee structures based on usage, customers began to take notice of their utility bills, and not in a good way. Many homeowners and business owners experienced steep increases in their bills without knowing why. When the confused customers called customer service for clarification, their questions often went unanswered. This process was reiterated in an article published by the *Wall Street Journal* which found that

> some utilities are falling down in the way they handle customer complaints and monitor data transmitted by the new digital meters... [the] commission to investigate the matter faulted the firm for doing too little to educate customers about the switch and for failing to respond to the full suite of data it gets from the meters.[11]

As a result, utility companies were put in the spotlight, needing to inform, educate and partner with their customers to provide the elevated levels of customer service.

The Los Angeles Department of Water and Power (LADWP) saw these changing mandates and knew improving communications by leveraging colour, relevancy and new statement design would address the challenges many of its peers were experiencing. However, the challenge for LADWP did not stop with customer service complaints. Through Assembly Bill 32, the State of California has charged each utility company with reducing carbon usage and greenhouse gas emissions (GHG) in order to increase conservation

FIGURE 6.7 LADWP old statement

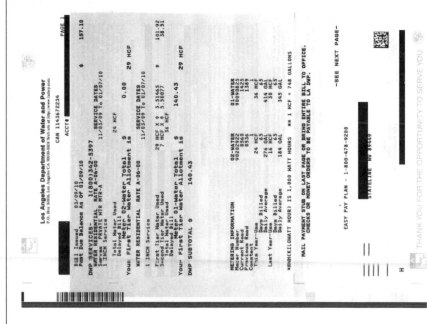

and reduce climate change. As a result of the State of California's environmental mandates, the mayor, LA City Council and LADWP convened to outline a plan and mitigate the rate impact of this bill. Rather than merely 'meet minimum' with these mandates and adhere to the required actions, the city of Los Angeles decided to strive for excellence and to become the cleanest city in the nation.

In order to accomplish this landmark initiative, LADWP needed its customers to reduce usage during peak hours, purchase Energy Star appliances and use only what they needed. The utility's primary communication channel was its billing statement. This required LADWP to reassess and redesign its customer statement to incorporate relevant, actionable messages in order to influence and change its customers' behaviours.

LADWP knew that education and engagement were required to gain its customers' trust and to build the partnerships the utility required for success. The utility delivers water and electricity to millions throughout the city of Los Angeles, making it the largest municipal utility in the United States. In addition to water and power services, LADWP also provides billing for the city's sanitation services (refuse disposal and sewerage).[12] With this robust customer base, LADWP engaged our team at InfoPrint to assist in the facilitation of these communication processes. Working with our team, LADWP's first step was to learn and understand its customer's expectations. As a result, LADWP conducted focus groups with external utility customers and also with internal LADWP personnel.[13]

In the light of LADWP's millions-strong customer base, simply surveying 1,000 customers or conducting a focus group with just a handful of residents would not have involved a sufficient sample size. Best practices dictate that the group design and selection must account for variations in demographics. Therefore, LADWP hosted several smaller focus groups in different neighbourhoods to ensure both demographic and geographic diversity. Because of the size and complexity of the Los Angeles area, capturing the perspectives of thousands of individuals in a rigorous manner was a daunting task.[14]

LADWP embraced this challenge. Its customers, call centre personnel and other key stakeholders provided valuable feedback regarding their difficulties with the existing LADWP statements. The focus groups offered suggestions to help the LADWP marketers and IT staff understand how to improve the readability of the statements. On the basis of the insights collected from the focus groups, new prototypes were created, reflecting the look and feel

FIGURE 6.8 LADWP statement

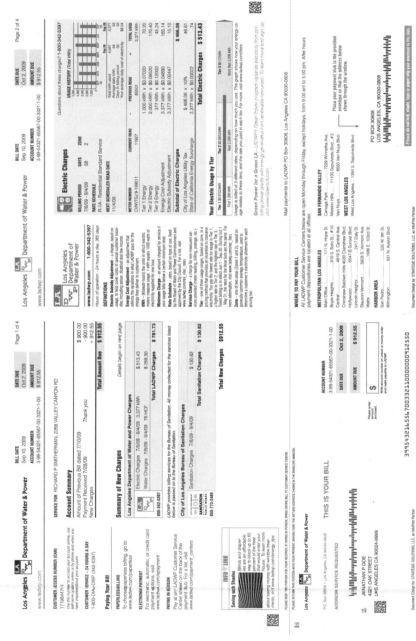

of the new billing statements. The prototypes were then shared with stake-holders and focus groups to validate and confirm that the new approach was on target with customer preferences.

The new statement features utility-based icons (an icon for power, an icon for water, an icon for trash, etc) together with aesthetically pleasing coloured graphs to show individual power consumption per home or busi-ness, allowing customers to more easily navigate their bill. These simple changes made it easier to distinguish refuse from sewerage, and water from electricity, enabling customers to more clearly understand the simple actions they can take to improve or change their energy usage. With this increased clarity, expensive call centre volume is expected to decrease as well.

Figures 6.8 and 6.9 offer a graphic depiction of LADWP's old statement design and new statement design.

Utilizing the Precision Marketing Framework, LADWP will have the ability to keep customers informed about what's most important to them: saving water, power and money.

Developing the right message

The right message is one that engages the customers and leads to behaviour that benefits both the customer and the company. That means crafting a message that is timely, specific to the customer and specific to the marketer's objectives, and that makes good use of the channel. Many of the examples in this book allude to examples of 'right messages', such as Royal Canin's individualized newsletters with information specific to the breed and age of the customer's dog; Amazon.com's 'people who bought X, also bought Y'; or Best Western's ability to reawaken 'sleeping beauties' in its loyalty programme with a 'More Rewards, Faster' campaign.

New channels and new methods help advertisers send the right message to the right people in ever more precise segments. For example, a website called One Day, One Job helps recent college graduates find jobs. The site uses Facebook as a platform because Facebook lets One Day, One Job post the candidate's job-wanted ads directly to Facebook users who self-identify as employees of particular companies. This lets job candidates potentially reach the right person. The experiences of some of One Day's clients illus-trate the power of the right message.

For example, one candidate created a very precisely targeted ad seeking a job at Disney and received 685 clicks, 21 e-mails, 4 Facebook messages

FIGURE 6.9 LADWP new statement: marketing pages

and a job interview at the company. In contrast, another candidate tried a less precise approach with an ad that went to 15 different companies. Although the ad got 50,992 views, it received only 117 clicks, and no job leads. The second candidate then tried a precise approach specifically targeting Sprint, which led to 5 e-mail contact leads. Overall, the One Day, One Job website has found that ads with very specific copy mentioning a specific company and sent to people affiliated with that specific company yields much better results than more generic copy.[15] In Precision Marketing, less is more, because it enables relevance.

Enabling more precise, relevant content in B2B

Business-to-business marketers face additional precision challenges compared to their business-to-consumer counterparts. A message can be highly relevant to the customer company but irrelevant to the particular employee receiving the message. Ted Vinzani, author of *RelevanceSells*, outlines the experience of one client, a company that sold repair, maintenance and cleaning services to grocery stores.[16] The company marketed these products to Maintenance supervisors. Then the company expanded into products that would improve store operations, such as special ethylene-absorbing filters that would significantly reduce the costs of spoilage of fresh flowers. But the Maintenance supervisors weren't interested in the more expensive filters, because spoilage was a Floral Department problem, not a Maintenance problem.

When the customer is a company, it's not the company that actually buys the product. Rather, it's specific people within the company who specify, select and approve the purchase of a product. Complex purchase processes mean marketers must send relevant messages that are precisely tuned to each person's role. Because each person has a specific role, relevant B2B marketing customizes the messages to those specific roles. For instance, someone in the Specification role might get technical messages about the features of products. In contrast, someone in a Budgeting or Approval role would get financial performance messages about the cost savings created by the company's product.

Using relevant rewards in your messaging

A large percentage of companies use rewards or discounts as a core part of their messaging and their loyalty programmes. Messages that communicate a discount, deal or free item can appeal to some customers. We are all familiar with the frequent-flyer-mile programmes, cashback credit cards and buy-10-get-one-free punch cards at the local coffee shops. In a survey of companies by the CMO Council, marketers cited discounts and savings (39.7 per cent of marketers), free products and premiums (34.4 per cent), and points for merchandise redemption (32.8 per cent) as key measurable member incentives for loyalty programmes.[17]

Media giant Bertelsmann uses customer data and information to add precisely customized rewards to its printed transactional communications.[18] Says Patrick Adams, SVP Interactive Customer Marketing, Bertelsmann Direct North America:

> Let's say you get an invoice from us and I want you to pay this invoice promptly. And let's say I know that you like a special author. I might communicate a message to say that if you pay this invoice by a certain date, I'll give you a promo code for a buy-one-get-one-free offer. Or, if I know that you are an avid reader of Stephen King, I might offer to put you at the top of the list on the pre-order list for Stephen King's next book.[19]

Non-monetary rewards: giving truly personal exclusives

Notice that the reward which Bertelsmann gives is, in some cases, not monetary. It costs Bertelsmann nothing to put a loyal customer at the top of the pre-order list. But because the message is precisely tuned and relevant to an avid fan, Bertelsmann knows that the customer will value the reward even if it costs nothing. Precision rewards can be – and perhaps should be – more about exclusivity and special service rather than just monetary rebate (except in the case of price-sensitive customers). As with gift-giving, it is the thought that counts, and Precision Marketing shows thought. When a company shows that it knows the customer's preferences and can offer something uniquely satisfying to that customer, then the exact monetary value is of lesser importance.

Overall, Bertelsmann found that precision communications always outperformed traditional mass marketing, and Adams feels that tailoring what the consumer sees is key to retention and loyalty:

> If you personalize the product they want to see, it's like night and day. Across the board, no matter what it is, if you're using a very basic level of customization or a more sophisticated level of customization it's always way more effective than just a real generic call or interaction.[20]

Measurable content

Given the increasing demand and pressure to deliver ROI, marketers and agencies continue to be under intense pressure to prove demonstrated results. Agencies must understand the metrics that will be used to gauge their success. In the Relevance Era, where relevance rules, only insight-driven campaigns, delivering irrefutable metrics and demonstrated ROI back to the business, will earn returns for the business and a credible seat for the Precision Marketer in the boardroom.

The Precision Marketer incorporates methods of measurement in the beginning of the creative and copy process rather than measurement being an afterthought when the programme launches. Metrics must be aligned and integrated into the fibre of the creative process and final design.

There are a few new tools that help facilitate the ease of measurement and assist in integrating offline with online for a true campaign view. For example, two popular tools, Quick Response (QR) codes and personal URLs, help to improve measurement and provide increased relevancy for customers.

A personal URL (PURL) is typically a website that contains some aspect of the customer's name. For example, a website may say '**www.leegallagher. precisionmarketer.com**', and when clicked, the website is customized to the customer. Traditionally, that click-through was tracked, and became the metric for a successful campaign. However, the fact of a customer simply visiting a site provides no information about what the customer actually did while visiting it. The Precision Marketer would use a visit to the personal URL to initiate a series of events that would further the customization and relevance of the engagement. For example, if Lee entered this site, which is customized similarly to others in his target segment, the website visit would trigger an e-mail to a sales call centre for further follow-up. Unlike many reporting vehicles, personal URLs allow for the drill-down of the customer's interest and are able to track site visits, downloads and other information that not only improves relevancy but also provides a rock-solid metric. Let's look at an example of them in action.

Example: how Babcock & Jenkins gathered data to craft personal messages

When customer-relationship marketing firm Babcock & Jenkins sought new clients, it researched each and every prospective customer: 641 executives from within certain industry segments. 'Our marketing department found facts relevant to that specific individual or that individual's organization as a way to show what our integrated approach could do,' says Lisa Blank, Marketing Manager at Babcock & Jenkins.[21]

The company then sent each executive a package of brownies accompanied by nothing more than a note with a PURL – a personalized URL. Upon visiting the PURL, each executive found a web page greeting him or her by name and with a personal and company-specific message such as 'Congratulations on [recipient's company's] second-quarter revenue growth!'[22]

Fully 43 per cent of the executives visited their PURL when they got the brownies, and 13 per cent requested 'Please contact me.'[23] The campaign was designed to showcase Babcock's relationship marketing services. 'Having a one-on-one dialog with that person – together with the personal URL, the facts about them, and addressing them by name – was the best way to showcase that.'[24] Using business customer data sources such as annual reports, industry media coverage, PR news and services such as Dun & Bradstreet lets B2B marketers gain critical insights into individual business customers.

A QR code is a two-dimensional bar code that, when scanned by a mobile phone camera, automatically and effortlessly directs the consumer to a designated point of interest on the internet. Recently, Ralph Lauren leveraged QR codes in a campaign to promote the US Open and drive traffic to its specific products, information and ordering on their website. What's more, QR codes have just skimmed the surface. According to Jonathan Bulkeley, then Chief Executive Officer of Scanbuy:

> You'll be able to walk past fruit at the supermarket, scan an apple, and see when it was picked and where it came from. While buying hair dye, you'll be able to scan the code on the signage and see instructions. You can create your own code, put it on a T-shirt, and then let people scan your shirt and link directly to your MySpace page.[25]

Imagine, just scanning with a mobile phone camera means that the code automatically directs the right person to the right product at the right time. QR codes and PURLS are valuable tools to a Precision Marketer's success. As the Ralph Lauren example points out, other tools will follow soon. In fact, Apple and Google are both developing the consumer response tag (CRT). This too will help the Precision Marketer to track, capture and learn about real customer behaviours so he or she can begin to determine how to better engage those customers with future content.

Strategies that succeed

Marketers play an increasingly valued role in their organizations when data-driven strategies are executed effectively and become the cornerstone of business results. As we have seen in this chapter, many companies today experience lacklustre campaign results that misallocate precious budget resources, alienate customers and offer little return back to the company. Most times, companies are not even aware of these misallocated spends because the metrics are not in place to deliver the insights needed to provide this knowledge. The ING example showed how one company had the knowledge, insight, passion and ability to evolve from old marketing habits and realign strategies that can be successfully implemented.

In the Precision Marketing Framework, future decisions are based on data. This effectively links financial results to business objectives. Aligning all strategies, tactics and measurements with the objectives means that the chances of success significantly improve. As we all know, some campaigns are more successful than others. If a lacklustre campaign occurs, you will now have collected data that will provide the necessary insight into improvement of the models, campaign and tactics. These measurements will allow you to successfully build and rebuild campaigns that steadily and iteratively improve over time.

A clear strategic approach from Step Four, Strategize, is the road map for a successful Precision Marketing deployment, which is where we will now move. Step Five, Deploy, is the 'move into action' phase of the Precision Marketing journey.

FIGURE 6.10 Precision Marketing Framework

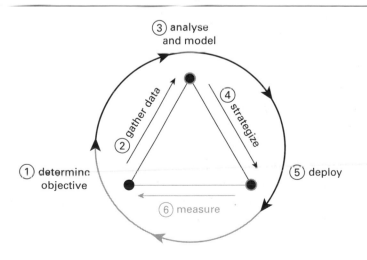

Key takeaway messages from Chapter 6,
'Step Four: Strategize'

- Using the fact-based output of analytics to develop a precisely targeted customer strategy is the key to planning and creating an effective Precision Marketing approach.

- Knowing which customers have the highest potential for both current and future revenue will help generate your highest return for marketing dollars spent. The categories we use are Low Propensity, Future Potential, High Propensity and Best Bets to describe the customer potential for revenue generation.

- The Strategize phase is the time to collaborate with your creative partners to generate relevant, customer-centric creative content.

- Use the Communication Matrix to align content to customers in order to keep customized, relevant content clearly mapped to customers.

- Marketers should play a strong role in developing fact-based strategic approaches, and Precision Marketing provides the tools and vehicles to enable marketers to do just that.

- Two popular tools, Quick Response (QR) codes and personal URLs, can be used to help improve measurement and provide increased relevancy for customers.

Notes

1   Alexander Hesse, Forrester Research, *ING Delivers Personalized Product Offers across Channels in Real Time*, 27 October 2009 [Online] **http://www.unica.com/documents/us/Unica_CaseStudy_ING_021910.pdf**.

2   Ibid.

3   Ibid.

4   Ibid.

5   Ibid.

6   Ibid.

7   CMO Council, *Why Relevance Drives Response and Relationships*, 2009.

8   CMO Council, *Routes to Revenue*, 2008 [Online] **http://www.dnblearningcenter.com/Whitepapers/Routes-to-Revenue-WhitePaper.pdf**.

9   Whitepaper, How to attract and retain customers with content now, Joe Pulizzi, Junta42.

10   Ibid.

11   Rebecca Smith, Probes find energy meters accurate, service lacking, *Wall Street Journal*, 7 September 2010.

12   Los Angeles Department of Water and Power chooses InfoPrint for next-generation communications infrastructure, *Printing Impressions*, 29 March 2010.

13   Ibid.

14   Infoprint.com, Case study: Los Angeles Department of Water and Power, 2010.

15   How 12 companies are leveraging the social network to advance their marketing objectives [Online] **http://www.slideshare.net/ralphpaglia/facebook-2562000**.

16   Ted Vinzani, Deny thy father and sell with relevance, Relevance Sells.com [Online] **http://www.relevancesells.com/2009/09/15/deny-thy-father-and-sell-with-relevance/**.

17   CMO Council, Loyalty leaders: Feeling the love from the loyalty clubs, 18 January 2009.

18   CMO Council, *Routes to Revenue*, 2008 [Online] **http://www.dnblearningcenter.com/Whitepapers/Routes-to-Revenue-WhitePaper.pdf**.

19   Ibid.

20   Ibid.

21   Kimberly Smith, Case study: How intrigue and personalization helped a marketing firm connect with handpicked leads, MarketingProfs.com, 21 October 2008 [Online] **http://www.marketingprofs.com/casestudy/111**.

22   Ibid.

23   Ibid.

24   Ibid.

25   Allen Stern, Polo Ralph Lauren launches QR code enabled mobile commerce site, CenterNetworks, 16 August 2008 [Online] **http://www.centernetworks.com/qr-code-mobile-commerce-ralph-lauren**.

Step Five: Deploy

> *Well done is better than well said.*
>
> **BENJAMIN FRANKLIN**

In this chapter, you will learn:

- how to deploy a Precision Marketing campaign;
- how to execute an in-market test;
- how to create a mobile marketing campaign;
- how to accelerate the deployment cycle.

While intelligent planning is an important foundation for the successful outcome of any project, action is the step that makes everything possible. Step Five, Deploy, is where the Precision Marketer moves into action. The case study of a large cable provider is a great way to show deployment in a real-world, practical example that produced stellar results.

Large cable provider takes action to sell VoIP

FIGURE 7.1 Large Cable Provider Overview

Large Cable Provider	
Objective:	Cross-selling VoIP services to its existing customer base
Strategy:	Target high-propensity customers recommended from the analysis phase with a relevant VoIP promotion
Tactics:	Integrate the relevant promotion into its must-read monthly cable to deliver the promotion
Results:	27% increase in the number of customers responding to the relevant colour

The Voice over Internet Protocol (VoIP) marketplace is increasingly crowded and fiercely competitive. Major telecom providers are using new fibre-optic networks with bundled offerings to quickly gain market share while other VoIP services providers, like Skype, are said to be growing at a rate of 380,000 users per day.[1]

In order to grow market share, one of the largest US cable providers set the objective of cross-selling VoIP services to its existing customer base. In the past, the cable provider had marketed all of its services to all of its customers and in all marketing channels, with billboards, television and direct mail topping the list.

Could this cable provider implement the Precision Marketing Framework to cross-sell its VoIP services by using targeted relevant promotions? Absolutely. Here's how.

Following the Precision Marketing Framework process, a meeting was set up to fully understand the objectives and explore the available data on hand. Once the data requirements were understood, transaction data were exported and provided to the InfoPrint data analytics team for analysis.

After careful review, 100,000 customers were selected to receive the targeted promotion for VoIP services. The strategy was to target high-propensity customers – who had been recommended from the analysis – with a relevant VoIP promotion.

Integrating the relevant promotion into the US cable provider's must-read monthly cable bill was the delivery tactic chosen. This was a different approach for the cable provider, which typically preferred direct mail for marketing. The promotional design would feature a well-known sports celebrity, and the creative copy would highlight the VoIP special offer. The full-page promotion was placed in the monthly bill and would engage the consumer because it would have to be paged through in order to see the monthly usage details.

Additionally, in order to measure the effects of colour, the promotion was produced in both full digital colour and monochrome to determine whether colour would help promote the call to action to subscribe to VoIP.

The in-market test consisted of two statistically equivalent groups of customers. The sample group consisted of 100,000 customers, of whom 50,000 would receive the colour cable promotion for VoIP and the other 50,000 would receive the same bill design and promotion printed in black and white. The monthly bills were sent out as usual and the measurement period was set for the following four weeks.

The cable provider experienced a 27 per cent increase in the number of customers responding to the relevant colour promotion. In addition, 50 per cent of the respondents who received the relevant colourful offer replied in the first two weeks of the four-week campaign. This is significant, as only 2 per cent of the customers who received the black-and-white offers replied in the first two weeks of the four-week campaign.

By following the Precision Marketing Framework, this large cable provider was able to increase responses to its VoIP services by leveraging its current customer base data to cross-sell other existing services. In the past, this company used its preferred communication channel, direct mail, to drive existing customers to buy additional services. This method was not driven by relevancy or even by who already had the product. Now, by implementing a few basic best practices rooted in data and metrics, this Precision Marketer has precisely achieved a significant return back to the company.

The campaign deployment

FIGURE 7.2 Step Five of the Precision Marketing Framework

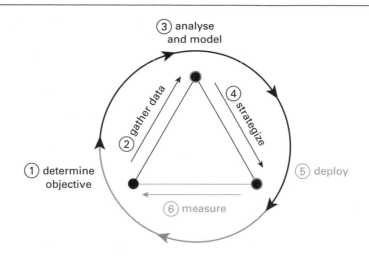

The Precision Marketing Framework's Deploy step focuses on managing and analysing the campaign performance to maximize effectiveness and optimize the ROI. The objectives have been determined, the analysis and modelling have been completed, the strategy has been communicated, and now the tactics need to be deployed.

In the Strategize step the tactics were chosen to integrate relevant messaging with the targeted customers in a way that could be measured. In the Deploy phase it is time to set up the delivery with the right rules to monitor the chosen channels (direct mail, e-mail, the web, etc). To reiterate, tracking mechanisms are particularly critical to the success of the campaign. Incorporating tracking codes or permanent identifiers into the design of the output will make it clear which messages or channels are driving the best responses and which ones are not working. Having this information will provide a distinct advantage for your analytical team and for your next campaign.

Deploying with precision in time

Timing can be everything; it can mean the difference between a wasted message that gets ignored and an embraced message that drives results. Precision

Marketing includes determining the precise timing of messages and offers so they have the greatest impact. For example, Harold's Chicken Shack wanted to reduce the afternoon sales slump between lunch and dinner. The company also wanted to get people in the habit of coming during these off-hours – eating lunch a little later, getting a mid-afternoon snack or coming for an early dinner.

Mobile marketing via Short Message Service (SMS) gave the restaurant chain the tools for Precision Marketing because most people look at a text message the instant they get it. But first, the company needed people to sign up to receive the messages. A wide range of more traditional marketing approaches drove opt-ins to a VIP programme. Harold's deployed calls to action on in-store signage (eg banners, counter flyers, table tents and window posters), on existing advertisements and other marketing efforts, such as door-to-door flyers in nearby neighbourhoods. Customers who signed up got an immediate 'thank-you' with an introductory message of 'Save 10% off your next meal Monday–Friday between 1 and 5 pm only. Bring a friend along and both of you save 20% each. Ends in 3 days. Exchangeable at local outlets.' The company then sent weekly messages with varying promotions designed to drive traffic during the usual slow periods and encourage a new behaviour in customers to visit during these slow times.

All participating stores shared a single short code, but each promotional message had a distinct keyword to track and understand response to their individual promotions. By tracking which codes drove redemptions, Harold's Chicken Shack was able to increase the precision of the SMS promotions in terms of both the timing of message delivery and the time limits on the offer. Overall, the best response came from messages delivered before noon and redeemable over a span of a few days.

Participating stores got 10,000 opt-ins during the first seven months. More than half (53 per cent) of the opt-ins redeemed the introductory coupon and nearly one-third (32 per cent) brought a friend. Subsequent promotions enjoyed a 37 per cent redemption rate, and the restaurant chain benefited from an 11 per cent lift in sales among participating outlets. 'We kept spending money on traditional marketing opportunities without any increasing result. Going with SMS coupons has given us an opportunity to connect with our customers anywhere and any time, and increase our sales during slow periods,' says Lawrence Nyong, a participating Harold's Chicken Shack owner.[2]

Full campaign deployment versus in-market test

Based on the campaign objectives, budgetary constraints and Precision Marketing expertise, there are several ways to implement and deploy your campaign – from a full-scale implementation for 100 per cent of your customers to an in-market test for a subset of your customer base. Once again we see that Precision Marketing is a journey. Starting smaller to test for expected and unexpected outcomes is a method to be preferred to, as some say, trying to boil the ocean. In-market tests provide a smaller-scale project with which to begin and from which to learn iteratively as you roll out and scale your deployment. Then, as your team builds its expertise and comfort levels with the Precision Marketing Framework, you can scale up and out for full implementation.

Executing your in-market test

In the simplest terms, an in-market test should be representative of how the campaign would perform on a national or even at a global level. The objectives selected in the in-market test need to align with the overall business objectives so that you can evaluate the performance of the test market.

Should the programme prove worthwhile on a smaller scale, the results will justify larger budgets or expanded support from the boardroom and executive team. If, when tested on a smaller scale, the programme shows unfavourable or unimpressive results, you have not spent your entire budget. Your resources can then be redeployed to other campaigns or in modifying and adjusting the current campaign.

Once the campaign content has been deployed, the in-market test will establish the baseline of the campaign. The outcomes or results of the in-market test provide insight on what performed well and what would need to be fine tuned. Regardless of the company size, in-market tests provide excellent learning opportunities. The Precision Marketer uses the six steps of the Precision Marketing Framework for this test, just as he or she would for a full implementation. Here is an example of how to conduct a simple in-market test.

Conducting a simple in-market testing

- *Step One: Define Your Objective.* This must reflect the business objectives of the larger campaign.

- *Step Two: Gather Data.* Gather data to support business needs or objectives. The data collected need to be similar to the aggregated collections of the larger campaign to ensure that the sampling and insight will be accurately conveyed when the campaign scales to a national or worldwide level.

- *Step Three: Analyse and Model.* Analyse and model the data with your analytics team. The analysis will help decide the best segments to test and geographies that best represent the overall outcomes of the campaign.

- *Step Four: Strategize.* Outline the strategy with specific metrics, measurements and timelines.

- *Step Five: Deploy.* Deploy the test to the channels that most represent the overall deployment strategy.

- *Step Six: Measure and Adjust.* We will cover this step in the following chapter in more detail, but it is necessary to measure the successes from your campaigns in order to effectively adjust for the full-scale implementation. If performed correctly, these results should reflect a snapshot of how the larger campaign would perform.

7-Eleven answers the phone

Customers' expectations have risen in recent years and their willingness to spend, generally speaking, has dropped. This is the 'new normal,' an economy that is much tighter and more constrained. Demand levels have fallen, thus requiring marketers to become much more sophisticated in terms of which customers to target and how to engage them. Marketers have no choice but to become better, more sophisticated, more tested marketers.

7-Eleven's mobile marketing campaign to promote its premier drinks is a good example of an in-market test, especially when deploying the ever-troublesome bar code on a mobile phone for redemption. In San Diego, approximately 200 7-Eleven convenience stores were testing a mobile marketing campaign in which consumers could send a text message to receive free coupons for their favourite beverages, such as a free Slurpee frozen carbonated beverage, Big Gulp fountain drink, fresh-brewed hot coffee and the latest proprietary drink, Iced Coffee.

Rita Bargerhuff, 7-Eleven Vice President and Chief Marketing Officer, says:

> 7-Eleven appeals to customers who are busy and on the go. Our marketing programs try to reach them where they are – by radio and outdoor when they're in the car, at movies and sporting events, or online at Facebook, Twitter and slurpee.com. Mobile marketing is the next step to reach our target customers – the millennials who don't go anywhere without their phones.

7-Eleven's primary objective was to test whether consumers would be comfortable using their phones to receive promotions. The secondary objective was to test whether this type of mobile programme would attract Generation Y/Millennial consumers, an extremely important yet elusive marketing segment for companies today.

According to Daniel May, Marketing Manager at 7-Eleven, this promotion was 7-Eleven's first effort with its new mobile marketing agency, GMR. The campaign was able to test several other elements of the promotion, including English/Spanish preference, media effectiveness, product-offering interest, redemptions verses participation, day part-participation, and phone and wireless carrier types. 'With the powerful metrics we can gather, we'll be able to better hone our mobile strategy for 2010,' May said. 'The mobile test with the optional opt-in gives us an opportunity to build a database of 7-Eleven customers through their most personal electronic device – their mobile phone.'

During the test, 7-Eleven shoppers would send a text with the word 'FAST' or 'RAPIDO' (fast in Spanish) to 72579. Then they would receive a message for a free beverage offer at 7-Eleven stores. The promotion was limited to one free beverage per day at participating 7-Eleven stores.

To redeem the offer, text message recipients with internet access on their phones could click through to a screen displaying a UPC bar code that could be scanned at the cash register. If customers did not have internet access, a 7-Eleven sales associate could enter the selected numeric code on the cash register for redemption.

The codes were good for the free beverage indicated in the coupon, and the message also included an invitation to receive future text messages with 7-Eleven news and offers. Recipients could opt in by replying 'YES', according to 7-Eleven.

'With the data captured in the campaign, we can continue to provide them with valuable offers and announcements of specials in the future,' May says. 7-Eleven clearly understands best practices in running in-market tests. Through careful planning and testing, 7-Eleven has avoided some of the read-rate accuracy problems that have plagued other retailers' trials and has delivered the right message to the right person at the right time.

Scaling for success

Rolling out the Precision Marketing Framework in a modular, scalable fashion requires planning. The Framework can be implemented quickly or over a long period of time as well as point to point, or across many campaigns. Many of our clients have implemented the Precision Marketing Framework in a matter of weeks to immediately drive incremental revenue back to the business.

Because the steps in the Precision Marketing Framework are cyclical, leading to continuous improvement, you can expand incrementally or move from the in-market test to full-scale campaigns. Each new programme or campaign sets the stage for the next one. Learning and refinement enable you to begin each new campaign in a stronger position than the one before. Each campaign generates new and valuable customer insights, enabling you to become more and more relevant to your customer.

In a 2009 survey by the CMO Council, nearly one-third (30 per cent) of consumers polled stated that they are inspired to do business with a company after receiving customized communications.[3] Through rigour and analysis, and by continually incorporating new insight, the Precision Marketer's programmes can produce the highest return.

Accelerating the deployment cycle at Max New York Life

Max New York Life (MNYL), a joint venture between Max India Ltd and New York Life International, created a rapid campaign deployment cycle with the objective of boosting sales to existing customers. 'Previously, we conducted two broadly targeted campaigns each quarter. Now, with these tightly defined customer segments, clean data, campaign management, and rapid modeling, we're executing 60 separate campaigns a month,' says Nagaiyan Karthikeyan, Head of Business Intelligence and Analytics.

Max New York Life now quickly tailors specific cross-sell offers and scripts different contact scenarios based on each customer's value, propensity to buy, propensity to pay and propensity to lapse. Karthikeyan explains, 'Now, we can build and run a model in two days. What's more, we're able to target our customer segments much more logically and granularly. We've identified about 25 separate cells, and we see their demographics and previous transaction behaviors.' The company uses SAS to aggregate and clean the data, build models, analyse datasets and manage campaigns.

Key elements of the new process included:

- a centralized repository of customer data;
- giving business users the right analytic tools to make good strategic decisions;
- a new technology foundation (SAS);
- clean contact data (addresses and phone numbers) to enable deployment of cross-selling campaigns.

With the new process, revenues from existing customers grew from 7 per cent to 20 per cent. 'Depending on how the macro economy performs, we think we can get that number closer to 25 percent or 30 percent. Our senior management team is very pleased with that performance,' says Karthikeyan. 'Sales cycles to existing customers are faster, and the average premium amount is often 30 percent to 40 percent higher. Plus, we've found that the retention probability for a customer goes up 300 percent to 400 percent once they make a second purchase with us.' High-margin revenue from cross-selling has tripled.[4]

The wrap

Regardless of the company size, in-market tests provide excellent learning opportunities to improve ongoing expansion of the project. The Precision Marketer uses the six steps of the Precision Marketing Framework to test and scale, in a monitored, managed and measured approach. As is demonstrated by the large cable company and 7-Eleven, if properly planned, many elements of the campaign can be tested for new insights before scaling the project. In the case of 7-Eleven, testing a new platform, such as mobile, was mandated because of the plethora of mobile phones available today, with different screen sizes, resolutions and operating systems. Careful planning, monitoring and measurements in both case studies provided successful outcomes back to their business.

So, what's the bottom line? If a company really wants to maximize its revenues, and especially its profits, it must think more holistically about the role of data, analytics and marketing messages. The Precision Marketing Framework ties marketing to measurable results. Lorrie Foster, VP of Councils and Research Working Groups at The Conference Board, said it best:

> In the past, marketing awareness and brand-building activities were enough
> to define marketing's mission and role in a company, and to justify its budget.
> Data and analytics let companies go beyond this qualitative approach. New
> approaches, methodologies and tools, and technologies are making it possible to
> link marketing investments directly to revenues and profits, holding marketing
> executives accountable for achieving expected results.

The next chapter, 'Step Six: Measure', discusses the quantifiable finish line that generates the objective, quantifiable metrics of success for a Precision Marketer.

Key takeaway messages from Chapter 7, 'Step Five: Deploy'

- There are several ways to implement and deploy – from a full-scale implementation for 100 per cent of your customers to an in-market test for a targeted subset of your customer base.

- An in-market test is an easier and more feasible way for many companies to start so that they can execute the Precision Marketing Framework, measure, learn and then iteratively expand the application of Precision Marketing across the entire marketing mix.

- An in-market test can be deployed using the same six steps of the Precision Marketing Framework to test your ideas and then scale them in a monitored, managed and measured approach.

- Precision Marketing includes determining the precise timing of messages so they have the greatest impact. Mobile marketing enables precision because most people look at a text message the instant they get it.

- Companies can accelerate the deployment cycle by scripting different offers and contact scenarios based on each customer's value, propensity to buy, propensity to pay and propensity to lapse.

Notes

1 Ross O. Storey, Skype growing by about 380,000 users a day, About.com, 10 February 2009 [Online] **http://pcworld.about.com/od/voip/ Skype-Growing-by-380-000-Users.htm**.

2 How 19 companies are boosting sales with SMS, mobile websites, mobile ads and Bluetooth marketing [Online] **http://www.slideshare.net/ sionner/marketing-profs-mobile-marketing-success-stories**.

3 CMO Council and InfoPrint Solutions, Why relevance drives response and relationships: using the power of Precision Marketing to better engage customers, 17 November 2009.

4 SAS® enables Max New York Life to maximize share of wallet, retain valuable customers [Online] **http://www.sas.com/success/mnyl.html**.

Step Six: Measure

> "What is now proved was once only imagined.
>
> **WILLIAM BLAKE**

In this chapter, you will learn:

- why measurement is important;
- how to set marketing metrics that align with strategic objectives;
- special considerations for B2B marketing.

A popular phrase is 'What gets measured, gets managed,' and that is true. However, in the world of marketing, even more than just measurement is required. Marketing metrics need to express objective, measurable results in the language of the business, such as revenue and ROI. Step Six, Measure, is all about producing the quantifiable results in the most relevant way: the language of the business. Our real-world example here is based on a highly metric-driven – and successful – company, Caesar's Entertainment.

Caesar's Entertainment

Remember when Rome fell? The equivalent shock happened in July 2004 when Harrah's Entertainment announced it would acquire Caesars Entertainment, an institution that once symbolized the glamour and wealth of Las Vegas.

With that impressive move, now rebranded as Caesar's became the single largest and most profitable gaming company in the world. The experience of Gary Loveman, mastermind of its path-breaking strategy, offers a glimpse of the true power of a data-driven enterprise intent on addressing its customers in the most relevant ways possible. The Caesar's example also demonstrates how feedback, monitoring and disciplined measurement can drive outstanding marketing and business results.

As you will see in this chapter, measurement is particularly critical to the success of a Precision Marketing programme. Measurement not only establishes accountability but also helps marketers identify which investments are paying off and which are not. In this final step of the Precision Marketing journey we move from Deployment back to Objective, and the vehicle that tells us how we did and what we should adjust is the Precision Marketing metrics. This is what we call the Measurement phase.

Back to Vegas for the moment. First, let's take a walk down the strip. You will be mesmerized by the visual delights all around you. You will see volcanoes erupting and pirate ships at war. You will be dazzled by extraordinary replicas of Paris, Venice and New York. And you will miss the point entirely.

Caesar's decided to forgo the flash. Instead, it decided to track and observe the behaviour of its customers. It actively accumulated customer spend data from its properties in Las Vegas, Atlantic City and many other locations to better understand its customers and their real desires. It then deployed this insight to test new marketing offers and provide individualized attention to these customers through its Total Rewards programme. It took calculated risks and broke the rules. Caesar's recognized that there was a hidden, unexplored reality that defied all conventional wisdom. The reality was that the most enduring profits were to be generated not by building grand amusements and catering to high-rollers, but rather by Caesar's personalizing its service to doctors, machinists, retired teachers and all other people who could be counted on to regularly enjoy a weekend of sensible gambling and entertainment.

Caesar's now manages 51 resorts across four continents. In a *Harvard Business Review* article, Caesar's CEO, Gary Loveman, stated that the company had strengthened customer loyalty and profitability in two key ways:

> First, we use database marketing and decision-science-based analytical tools to widen the gap between us and casino operators who base their customer incentives more on intuition than evidence. Second, we deliver the great service that consumers demand. In short, we've come out on top in the casino wars by mining our customer data deeply, running market experiments, and using the

results to develop and implement finely tuned marketing and service-delivery strategies that keep our customers coming back.[1]

One interesting example of the company's effective use of feedback is its ability to engage in 'marketing interventions' on the gaming floor. Should a valued patron experience losses at the gaming tables that reach a certain threshold or 'pain point,' the casino dispatches a 'luck ambassador' to offer the gambler a special reward, say tickets to a show or a dinner for two – a measure that is matched to the individual's particular profile of interests and preferences.

David Norton, Caesar's Chief Marketing Officer, is now challenged to defend the company's enormous winnings in an extremely challenging economy. Fortunately, he has the data and the metrics to do so. In 2009, Norton and his colleagues set out to simultaneously deliver both cost containment and revenue growth across Caesar's many resort properties worldwide and $10 billion in revenues.[2] Norton says:

> The senior management team knew we had to get the cost of ineffective direct-marketing expense out of the system with the understanding that consumers were responding differently in the new world order. However, we had to be very surgical in our approach at a program and segment level. Our execution plan was the key to our success as we mandated control groups for all programs, centralized marketing analysis so that we would better understand which programs were driving incremental profitability, and enhanced management reporting so that nonconformers could be dealt with.[3]

The company also had to find new sources of growth. '[W]e had to stimulate new revenue through a couple of projects that we were willing to make a strategic bet on based on analytics and research,' Norton adds. 'Effective implementation was critical here, too, in order to gain buy in and quickly generate the returns we anticipated.'[4]

The company's Total Rewards loyalty programme has proved particularly valuable in terms of enabling the company to measure the impact of its marketing investments and produce new revenue through its findings. The loyalty programme enables the company to collect data on how often programme members visit the company's properties, where and how they are spending money, how profitable they are as customers, and what types of gaming and entertainment experiences they value most.

Such insights drive more relevance in marketing and more revenue to the business. 'If we know a player has been to past slot tournaments, we'll make sure he or she gets invited to the next one,' says Norton. 'If they've never come to a mid-week event, we exclude them from mailings about mid-week events because, obviously, they're not going to respond.'[5]

According to Norton, Caesar's now tracks 80 per cent of customer spend through the Total Rewards card programme, tracking 40 million casino customers. Harrah's uses those customer data extensively, and the extremely positive outcomes have helped Caesar's expand and grow profitably. Caesar's success recently helped Norton become *Target Marketing* magazine's Direct Marketer of the Year.[6]

What were the measurable results for Caesar's? –

- identified a new customer segment: 0.15% of customers generate an amazing 12% of Harrah's revenue;
- generated cost savings of $15–20 million by centralizing marketing analytics;
- expanded its number of properties during Norton's 12-year tenure from 15 to 52.

Regarding measurement of direct marketing efforts, Norton sums it up best by saying, 'Everybody can have an opinion, but the beauty of direct marketing (measurement) is we'll know who was right.'

As the Caesar's example demonstrates, marketers who have a tight handle on their metrics are in a position to take action when the business environment changes. They can move to contain costs and increase investments, relying on their analysis and reporting to justify their actions.

What gets measured gets managed

As the economic environment has become more challenging and competition for budget dollars has intensified, the pressure on marketers to demonstrate a return on their marketing investments is now a mandate. Demonstrating marketing's value to the business has only grown, further emphasizing the need for Precision Marketing.

While studies of the CEO's agenda have consistently shown a focus on top-line growth and customer retention as core imperatives, marketers often seem to have relatively misaligned priorities. In one study, Booz Allen and the Association of National Advertisers found that 83 per cent of the marketing respondents were focused on branding as opposed to producing growth (47 per cent).[7]

To achieve greater credibility, chief marketing officers (CMOs) are under pressure to align not only with the CEO but with the chief financial officer (CFO) as well. Too often, marketing and finance don't speak the same language. While marketing talks creativity, finance talks bottom line. They are both mystified by the other's perspectives. The finance group trumps marketing because the bottom line, revenue and ROI – not creativity and branding – are the language of the business.

Marketing's methods and measurements will continue to lack credibility throughout the executive suite if these barriers are not overcome. Precision Marketing brings the tools to build the bridges required to span the barriers. The CFO is responsible for budgeting and is expected to closely analyse and evaluate the returns on all significant corporate expenditures. Should marketing remain out of sync with the plans and projections developed by finance, then marketing will continue to lose budgetary support and credibility. Keeping both objective credibility and marketing budgets intact is one factor driving growing commitment to measurement on marketing's part.

Marketing leaders and managers should not be merely (or primarily) motivated by fear. As successful marketers at firms like Tesco, ING and Caesar's have clearly demonstrated, solid measurement is the driver of superior marketing performance. Precision is the best measurement for showing marketing's impact on growth and improving one's career prospects in the process.

Marketers must have the ability to speak to how investments in marketing drive top-line revenue. Marketers need to know and consistently report and communicate the ROI associated with each individual campaign, programme and initiative. Like those in every other area of the business, marketers must shift the budget towards activities that deliver maximum, measurable returns. This is how marketers divest themselves of non-measurable activities that represent a needless drain on resources. This is how marketers set the stage for clear and impressive marketing performance. And this is how marketers continue the Precision Marketing journey.

To underscore the importance of marketing measurement and accountability, Norton of Caesar's states, 'We've made this very much a marketing company. So for better or worse, when performance isn't there, people look to marketing. And when things are going pretty well, people look to marketing as well. So I think that's a positive.'[8]

What gets measured gets managed. The measured results become the focus of attention, the driver of investment and the means by which marketers track progress and performance. To a Precision Marketer, objective, factual measurement is one of the core drivers of credibility and the scorecard for directing future action.

The Measurement Phase

FIGURE 8.1 Step Six of the Precision Marketing Framework

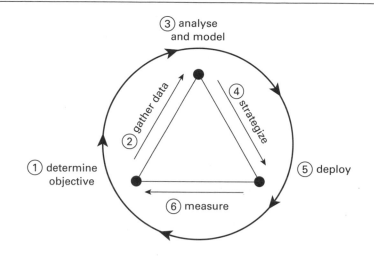

The final leg of the Precision Marketing journey, the Measurement phase, is where marketers demonstrate the impact of their efforts. The Measurement phase takes marketers from Deployment back to Objective. Measurement is the means by which marketers demonstrate that they are aligned with the goals, objectives and imperatives of the business and scores marketing's results and contributions relative to those business goals. Measurement is the mechanism for quantifying – in a clear, factual and transparent fashion – the impact of the marketing investments.

Measurement is also the key to establishing accountability for actions and outcomes. To reiterate, if marketers are to receive the financial backing of the organization, as well as recognition for their impact on revenue, they will have to be disciplined in the measurement of programmes and campaigns. They will have to report clearly measured results and to communicate the impact of those results effectively.

What should marketers be measuring?

In the past, there has long been a commitment among some marketers to measure 'awareness' metrics, counting everything from media mentions to brand survey responses. Direct marketers, who drove the growth of direct mail, rose to prominence in the field in the 1980s. They introduced an array of new metrics around recency, frequency and monetary (RFM) factors, and in many cases were able to close the loop between investment and impact. Closing that loop was one of the precursors of Precision Marketing.

Today the environment is far more complex. There has been a proliferation of channels and media over the years, and buyer behaviour has become far less predictable. Shoppers are now engaging in research in one channel but often purchasing in a different channel, thus increasing marketers' need to analyse, predict and measure customer behaviours. Under these circumstances, there is a need to be clear in terms of what is measured and what these metrics support. While in recent years there has been a great deal of attention placed on web-based metrics such as unique visitors, hits and click-through rates, it is important to recognize that these are merely intermediary metrics. They certainly do not speak the language of the C-Suite. They don't tell you how marketing investments are influencing revenue or driving sales. That is not to say these metrics are not helpful, just that they are intermediary.

Many metrics represent leading indicators of what is to come. These metrics can guide investments and help allocate the spread around different channels in a company's portfolio.

First, metrics should ultimately relate to the objectives determined at the outset of the Precision Marketing initiative. As has been discussed in prior chapters, plans will tend to revolve around one or more of four possible objectives:

- customer retention;
- customer growth;
- customer reactivation;
- customer acquisition.

Most often, metrics that capture customer response rates, customer conversion rates and revenue generated will form the foundational metrics across these four objectives.

Second, metrics are often built around industry-specific and business-specific dynamics. For example, in the hospitality industry metrics might include number of stays per year, number of nights stayed per visit and revenue spent per visit. In the insurance industry, metrics might include number of insurance products per customer, payment time per customer, number of customer lapses, and so forth.

Comparing Precision Marketing metrics to a statistically balanced and sized control group is essential to generating the measurable uptick associated with your Precision Marketing initiative. This comparison will gauge the real return on your Precision Marketing investments and continue the journey and expansion across your customer touchpoints. As already mentioned, in the customer implementations we have worked on, not one company has abandoned the Precision Marketing Framework.

The Measurement phase is the finish line that sets the stage for the next Precision Marketing implementation and/or expansion. Typically, you will set several metrics at the beginning of the initiative. In the Measurement phase you generate and analyse the data that create your Precision Marketing scorecard. Let's look at a few more real-world examples: Starwood Vacation Ownership and the Nationwide Building Society.

Gearing up for growth

One metric that is often tracked is the effectiveness of cross-sell or up-sell campaigns, offers and interactions. Response and conversion rates are considered important metrics that must be known.

Starwood Vacation Ownership, a wholly owned subsidiary of Starwood Hotels and Resorts Worldwide, was intent on cross-selling the company's vacation resort offerings to existing customers of the Starwood brand. Starwood Vacation Ownership's direct marketing team was charged with maintaining the organization's growth by leveraging such assets as the Starwood Preferred Guest loyalty programme. 'In our business, making sales begins with gaining a deep understanding of each individual customer,' says Ron Lange, Senior Marketing Database Manager.[9]

The company offers 'vacation ownership interval' programmes enabling customers to spend a week in a particular destination, and 'fractional ownership' programmes that provide a three- to six-week stay at an upscale, luxury property. 'Each of these customer experiences appeals to different buyers,' Lange adds, explaining that the challenge is to determine the likely receptivity of particular customers to particular vacation offers.

Leveraging its investments in customer insight and marketing automation from Unica, Starwood Vacation Ownership drove customer growth to new levels through insight-driven cross-selling. The company, for instance, is now able to determine whether a customer has stayed at a Westin hotel on a particular Caribbean island and then present an offer for a vacation property on the same island.

As the evidence shows, Starwood Vacation Ownership's measures are on the mark. Through investments in Precision Marketing the company increased response rates by 15 per cent and booking rates by 24 per cent in the first six months of its programme. The company was also able to reach customers who had booked packages but not yet scheduled them, boosting activation rates by 20 per cent within a given arrival time (Figure 8.2). Tracking the results of its campaigns helps Starwood marketers to document the results they delivered and to set the stage for future Precision Marketing efforts.

FIGURE 8.2 Standard Vacation Ownership Precision Marketing Results

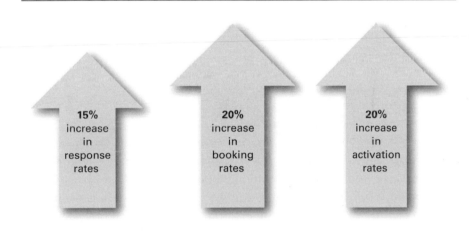

15% increase in response rates

20% increase in booking rates

20% increase in activation rates

The Nationwide Building Society builds relationships

In another example, Britain's Nationwide Building Society, a full-service financial services provider and the world's largest building society, shows how active measurement and tracking can enhance the precision and performance of a company's marketing strategy or plan.

Recognizing that highly personalized service was the key to reducing churn and strengthening profitability, the organization launched an extensive customer initiative to connect with its 11 million customers in a more engaging and profitable fashion. The company actively tracked retention rates as well as cross-sell numbers to ensure its initiatives were delivering expected returns.

Nationwide Building Society's advanced customer interaction solution guides its customer-facing representatives through each customer conversation with intelligent prompts. Relying on real-time guidance, the organization has enhanced both cross-selling and customer care. Simon Baines, Nationwide's Head of Customer Insight, says:

> We wanted to ensure that we could show our customers that we knew who they were, respond quickly and professionally to meet their needs and ensure that we were able to take the opportunities to strengthen relationships. To do this we needed to ensure we only offered things to customers that we knew would be relevant to them.[10]

The results? The organization has achieved sales of over 200 per cent of predicted levels. Whether customers were engaged in a branch, on the website or via the call centre, they experienced a seamless and personalized interaction. Nationwide, which wanted to differentiate itself in a crowded, competitive market, has met its objectives and further strengthened its revenue and its brand.[11]

Metrics for B2B marketing

Many marketers on the B2B side get mired in operational metrics such as impressions and click-throughs because they view their jobs as sales-lead generation. Instead, they should be looking at longer-term metrics.

Polycom, a provider of communications technology to businesses, runs a robust B2B marketing effort that includes targeted e-mail campaigns, trade shows, public relations and an online presence. As its CMO, Heidi Melin, says:

> We have a platform that measures all the responses that come into the top of our funnel and tracks them all the way to closing business. We've found, for example, that trade shows generate a lot of contacts, but the business closed is not as high as a targeted e-mail campaign into our installed customer base.[12]

Coming full circle

Running pilots and small in-market tests enables companies to learn. As has been mentioned, it is highly recommended to measure Precision Marketing campaigns in a test versus control group to gauge the true increase in return from Precision Marketing compared with the status quo. Experiments – tests and trials – may not deliver successful outcomes, but they always produce findings that can drive new learning. More importantly, they can help avoid vast misallocations of marketing capital.

Through trial and error, you'll learn where the most significant opportunities lie and what actions should be taken to maximize returns. Capital One became famous for running as many as 80,000 tests annually, helping the company become the United States' fifth-largest provider of credit cards and setting the stage for its more recent moves into full-service banking.

Rich Fairbank, the company's co-founder, once said he was attracted to the credit card industry because of its 'ability to turn a business into a scientific laboratory where every decision about product design, marketing, channels of communication, credit lines, customer selection, collection policies and cross-selling decisions could be subjected to systematic testing using thousands of experiments.'[13] That spirit is now pervading other industries in a big way – everything from utilities to telecommunications to hospitality to retail. It is this commitment to data-driven approaches – to rigour and discipline – that is behind the emergence of Precision Marketing.

By making new discoveries and attaching measurable results to those findings, marketing will contribute more to the company's success. Customer insights and ability to engage your customers in more relevant ways will help increase the value that marketing holds for your organization's growth strategy in the coming years. And this will be made possible through measurement, which is the ultimate scorekeeper on success.

Congratulations – you have completed your first Precision Marketing journey. From here, you are ready to take what you have learned and apply it to your next Precision Marketing initiative. You are now ready to return to Step One and expand your application of Precision Marketing.

FIGURE 8.3 Precision Marketing Framework

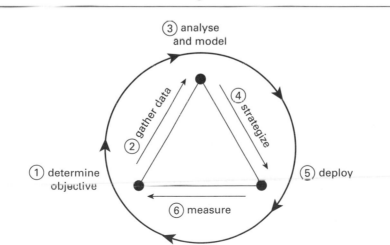

> Key takeaway messages from Chapter 8, 'Step Six: Measure'
>
> - Pressure on marketers to demonstrate a return on their marketing investments is intensifying. Marketing metrics need to express objective, measurable results in the language of the business such as revenue and ROI.
>
> - Measurement is where the Precision Marketing Framework comes full circle and allows a factual summary of results to assist you in setting up the next deployment of Precision Marketing in a smarter, broader fashion.
>
> - B2B marketers need to move away from operational metrics and move towards looking at longer-term metrics such as the total value of a customer from marketing activities.
>
> - What gets measured gets managed. The measured results become the focus of attention, the driver of investment, and the means by which marketers track progress and performance. To a Precision Marketer, objective, factual measurement is one of the core drivers of credibility and the scorecard for directing future action.
>
> - Comparing Precision Marketing metrics to a statistically balanced and sized control group is essential to generating the measurable uptick associated with your Precision Marketing initiative. This comparison will gauge the real return on your Precision Marketing investments.

Notes

1 Gary Loveman, Diamonds in the data mine, *Harvard Business Review*, May 2003.

2 *Target Marketing* magazine, October 2010.

3 CMO.com, A conversation with 'CMO of the Year' finalist David Norton, Harrah's Entertainment, 10 May 2010.

4 Ibid.

5 Ibid.

6 Heather Fletcher, Direct Marketer of the Year: David Norton, *Target Marketing*, October 2010.

7 Are CMOs irrelevant? Organization, value, accountability, and the new marketing agenda, Booz Allen.com, 2004.

8 Heather Fletcher, Direct Marketer of the Year: David Norton, *Target Marketing*, October 2010.

9 Unica.com, Case study: Starwood Vacation Ownership, 2010.

10 Portraitsoftware.com, Case study: Nationwide Building Society, 2010.

11 Ibid.

12 Jon VanZile, Judging marketing metrics, 7 December 2009 [Online] **http://www.btobonline.com/article/20091207/FREE/912039995/ judging-marketing-metrics#seenit**.

13 Thomas H Davenport, How to design smart business experiments, *Harvard Business Review*, February 2009.

Targeted Tesco

> *If you want to know your past, look into your present conditions. If you want to know your future, look into your present actions.*
>
> **ANONYMOUS**

In this chapter, you will learn:

- how the entire six-step Precision Marketing Framework can be executed, by following an in-depth case study of one company's Precision Marketing journey.

The path through the Precision Marketing Framework is a journey, so it is helpful to have the end goal consistently in sight. Tesco's story of success closely follows the Precision Marketing Framework. In this chapter we show how Tesco embarked on its journey.

Step One: Define Your Objective

In its early days, Tesco was known as the low-price grocery store. In the early 1990s, Tesco was losing customers to competitors, and Tesco executives realized that a low-cost strategy by itself was not sustainable. Retaining its loyal customers became Tesco's primary objective. In addition to customer retention, Tesco also needed to focus on customer growth and customer reactivation.

Step Two: Gather Data

Quick survey

In order to achieve its objective, Tesco needed to understand who its loyal customers were, what their profiles looked like and whom they should target with which offers. In order to gain these insights, its executives needed to collect data. Tesco developed its Clubcard service to begin the data collection process. The Clubcard application form captures the customer's name, address and phone number. It also asks a bare minimum of details about the customer's household, the number of people in the household and a simple list of a few dietary preferences for each household member. The form's dietary preference check-boxes help Tesco avoid strong marketing turn-offs such as promoting wine to a teetotaller or pork to someone who observes a kosher diet.

Tesco then offers a set of six optional 'Clubs' such as a cooking-oriented food club, a wine club, a healthy living club, a baby and toddler club, a Christmas saving club and a greener living club. When a customer joins one of these clubs, Tesco gets to know more about the customer, for example, if they join the baby and toddler club the fact that they have young children.[1]

Finally, the application asks a few personal preference questions about how Tesco is permitted to use the customer's data.[2]

The Clubcard rewards Tesco customers by offering special vouchers and extra points. Every time the card vouchers are used, Tesco is able to collect information on its customers' buying patterns and preferences. While the customer earns points, Tesco earns information.

Transaction data collection

The information collected on the Clubcard application represents only a tiny start in Tesco's quest for data. Knowing where someone lives or the ages of people in the household is not sufficient to predict behaviour. Tesco finds the rich relevance-generating data in the transactions at the cash register, which provide real-world customer behaviours. With over 200 million purchases recorded on Clubcard weekly, Tesco is collecting staggering amounts of data.[3] Every time customers use their Clubcard they earn bonus points, which they accumulate to redeem rewards. Tesco, in turn, uses the opportunity to gather data on the customer's purchase and to connect each customer's shopping basket with every other time that Clubcard member has shopped at Tesco.

Step Three: Analyse and Model

When launching Clubcard, Tesco tapped a small marketing predictive analytics firm, Dunnhumby, to help with data analytics. Today, Dunnhumby processes the data that flood in from thousands of stores and millions of shoppers. This system handles billions of pieces of data on who bought what, when, where, and with what promotions. Although it seems like an overwhelming amount of data, Dunnhumby found that it did not need to process all these data. Taking a sample of only 10 per cent of the data gives results to 90 per cent accuracy.[4] Processing all of the data, a task more than 10 times as complex, might only raise accuracy by a small amount. Dunnhumby found that sometimes less is good enough.

Tesco liked the results so much that it eventually bought 83 per cent of Dunnhumby. Despite the fact that Tesco is the majority owner, Dunnhumby continues to do work for other companies such as Kroger, Groupe Casino, Gillette, P&G, GlaxoSmithKline, Müller, Nestlé, Unilever and Coca-Cola.[5]

Segment products to allow match-up to customers

Tesco's analysis process starts with a multidimensional description of each product and consists of the 50,000 products found in Tesco stores. Dimensions include attributes such as:

- relative price (from least to most expensive);
- branding (from Tesco's house brand to national brands);
- ethnicity (from traditional to ethnic).

Tesco uses a total of 20 different dimensions to create a more meaningful description for the types of products bought by Clubcard members.[6] By characterizing products on a meaningful set of dimensions, Tesco can segment customers on the general kinds of products they buy rather than the overly detailed specifics of what they buy.

Segmenting and profiling customers

Tesco then clusters its customers into segments based on the kinds of products they buy. Overall, Tesco found that its Clubcard customers fall into six top-level segments with varying percentages of customers in each segment:[7]

- Finer Food: 19% of customers;
- Healthy Eaters: 17% of customers;
- Traditional: 15% of customers;
- Convenience: 9% of customers;
- Mainstream: 24% of customers;
- Price Sensitive: 16% of customers.

Tesco further subdivides customers into as many as 20,000 segments. These segments go beyond standard demographic and geographic segments to reveal, for example, whether the member has a baby or a pet, and whether he or she cooks often or doesn't cook at all.[8] Then, when designing messages that promote products which a particular customer has never bought before, Tesco uses profiling. Tesco looks at the items found in other shopping baskets of customers who are similar to the target customer. This is how Tesco predicts what the target customer might like that they have never bought before.

Analyse voucher-usage behaviour

Tesco monitors voucher use to understand which customers use which voucher and when. These analyses help Tesco further segment customers or increase relevancy through new programmes. For example, Andrew Mann, former Marketing Director of Clubcard, says, 'Our data helped us to identify a group of customers who were not using vouchers regularly, but who were saving them and spending them in bulk in the run up to Christmas.' Tesco created a special Christmas Savers Club programme for these people, whereby Tesco saves the vouchers and sends a special mailing to Christmas Savers Club members. 'The Savers Club means customers don't lose out if they have stored their vouchers over the year and, for example, have misplaced them.'[9]

Step Four: Strategize

Retaining its loyal customers became Tesco's primary objective, with a secondary focus on customer growth and acquisition. To gain a deeper understanding of its customers, Tesco leveraged Dunnhumby to provide product recommendations, segmenting and predictive behaviours.

Now Tesco needed to devise strategies that would create the best out-come to achieve its objectives. Tesco decided to make specific offers based on the customer goal. For example:

- *Customer retention*. Reward with a coupon for a product the customer buys often.

- *Customer reactivation*. Discount an item that the customer has bought in the past but not recently.

- *Customer growth*. Use cross-selling tactics to promote a new item that the customer has never bought but might like (according to the data within the customer database).

Customer retention: give to get

Tesco sends reward vouchers that give the customer a discount on those products that the customer buys often. Although giving away a discount on what the customer buys anyway may seem like a money-loser, it is actually a way that Tesco builds relevance for the entire Clubcard system. Tesco views these vouchers as a little quarterly reward, to thank its customers for their participation in the Clubcard programme. In turn, customers know that every mailing contains some satisfying sure bets and they are therefore much more likely to read and respond to Tesco's marketing messages.

Customer reactivation: promote to retain loyalty

Other vouchers Tesco delivers cover items that the customer seems to have stopped buying. If a customer consistently buys a particular product month after month and then stops, Tesco sees if a little promotion might help. These 'please come back' promotions help retain customers as well as reac-tivate their spending habits by ensuring that the customer's business doesn't slowly trickle away to competitors.

Customer growth: cross-sell to build loyalty and revenue

Clubcard members also receive offers for products that they have not pur-chased but which, on the basis of predictive analytics, Tesco believes, they might like. These cross-selling promotions include two categories of goods.

First, they include key staples that virtually everyone needs but which this customer is not buying from Tesco. For example, Tesco might notice that a customer is not buying any bread and infer that the customer must be buying it elsewhere (eg at a different bakery).[10] A promotional voucher for Tesco's own in-house bakery might entice that customer to switch or come back to Tesco. Second, Tesco might offer a voucher on a product that it believes the customer might like, on the basis of previous purchases and what Tesco knows about the customer. These might be new products or products bought by other customers who match the profile of the target customer.

Step Five: Deploy

Fourteen million variations of loyalty

Let's look in detail at how Tesco achieves its superior direct mail results. Every three months Tesco sends every Clubcard member a direct mailing. Tesco's Clubcard 'has a core proposition – to create value for customers and lifetime loyalty, and our quarterly statements are the heart of this,' said Mann, then a marketing director of Clubcard.[11] Tesco creates value and relevance by personalizing each mailing using Clubcard data and extensive analytics. The result is 14 million variations each quarter. The week these promotions are mailed, they account for a quarter of all postal deliveries.[12] Using a data-driven approach, Tesco can tailor promotions to individual shoppers and quickly determine whether the promotion is working.

For example, Tesco's quarterly mailing includes a Clubcard statement, vouchers for Clubcard rewards, which are worth between 1 per cent and 4 per cent of the customer's spending during the quarter, and various promotions for various products. What is different about Tesco is that it does not just blast customers with a random selection of promotions or a cookie-cutter spread of coupons. 'We are using our data to identify precisely what they buy and to target relevant offers. For example, there's no point in offering vouchers for red wine if the customer predominantly drinks white, or promoting deals on French wine if they prefer Italian,' Mann said.[13] Clubcard vouchers provide discounts on three types of carefully selected products that Tesco picks for their likely relevance to that particular customer.

Step Six: Measure

As we have seen with many cases throughout this book, companies use the data collected in many non-traditional ways. The Oakland A's found undervalued players, Caesar's found undervalued customers and the large hotel chain found undervalued groups of customers. Tesco uses its data in both traditional and non-traditional ways.

Many ask: how much can relevancy-based marketing lift a company's sales, in the best case? To answer this question, companies need to understand how much more a customer might buy that they do not already buy. The same transaction data that a company like Tesco uses to estimate loyalty can also help understand the 'headroom' with each customer, or the potential amount of additional sales with that customer.

In Tesco's case the company knows how many people live in the shopper's household and their approximate ages. Tesco then multiplies the household size by the calorie needs of the average person of each age. The result is a rough estimate of how much food that household might eat each week. Tesco then compares what the family probably eats with what Tesco knows they buy at Tesco. The difference tells Tesco about the potential opportunity. This estimate will never be exact because some people eat more or less than others. However, if a family of five only seems to buy enough food for one person, Tesco knows it has some headroom for expanding sales to that customer. Headroom estimates help Tesco in two ways: 1) to know which customers to target; and 2) to help create predicted ROI for any marketing campaign.

Tesco illustrates what a company can do with a highly relevant strategy of messaging and personalized promotions:

- Clubcard now totals some 16 million active members in the United Kingdom, which represents half of all British households, and an average of over 7,000 Clubcard members for each of Tesco's 2,000 UK stores.[14]

- Clubcard also enjoys a strong following in the 12 other countries in which Tesco operates. Another 12.5 million active international members represent an average of over 12,000 Clubcard members for each of Tesco's 1,000 non-UK stores. In fact, when Tesco launched Clubcard in Poland, Thailand and Slovakia, 3 million new card-holders joined in only seven weeks.[15]

- The fact that 1,000 Clubcard members call every day to report a change of address is further evidence of how important the Clubcard mailings are to the members.[16]

- Tesco's targeted Clubcard promotions enjoy redemption rates in the 20–40% range.[17] What is even more impressive is that Tesco quarterly vouchers have a redemption rate of 98.4%, while the industry average for opened direct mail is a measly 1%.[18]

Having changed from being a 'pile it high' commodity grocer to a data-driven, customer-centric company, Tesco is now one of the largest grocery chains in the world, with the most loyal followers. Tesco's vision to create and leverage its data to improve customer understanding has now resulted in its data becoming one of the most valuable assets to the company. Through constant adjustment and modifications for more than 15 years, Tesco continues to deliver relevant communications to its customers, grow market share, expand into new markets and increase revenue.

The path through the Precision Marketing Framework is a journey, and it is helpful to have the end goal in sight. Tesco's story clearly demonstrates the powerful transformation that can occur when using data-driven insights to deliver the right message to the right person at the right time in the right channel.

Key takeaway messages from Chapter 9, 'Targeted Tesco'

- We began the Precision Marketing journey by discussing Tesco's data-driven approaches, which provided demonstrated returns back to the company.

- Tesco excelled at using methods similar to the Precision Marketing Framework. It defined its objectives, learned that it needed to collect and gather data, then analysed and created models to uncover the best way to communicate with distinct and diverse customer segments. Tesco delivered relevant, meaningful communications to its customers and tracked its successes.

- Through constant adjustment and modifications for more than 15 years, Tesco has continued to deliver relevant communications to its customers, grow market share, expand into new markets and increase its revenue.

- Now the United Kingdom's largest retailer, Tesco shows the proven value of the Precision Marketing Framework.

Notes

1 http://www.tesco.com.

2 Ibid.

3 BIMA, Tesco Clubcard [Online] http://www.bima.co.uk/
   membershowcase/44/ehs-4d-group/tesco-Clubcard/.

4 *Marketing Magazine*, Scoring points as Tesco Clubcard hits 10,
   2 October 2003 [Online] http://www.marketingmagazine.co.uk/
   news/191867/Scoring-points-Tesco-Clubcard-hits-10.

5 http://www.dunnhumby.com.

6 Clive Humby and Terry Hunt with Tim Phillips, *Scoring Points*, Kogan Page,
   London, 2003.

7 Coriolis Research, Tesco: A case study in supermarket excellence, 2004
   [Online] http://www.coriolisresearch.com/pdfs/
   coriolis_tesco_study_in_excellence.pdf.

8 Graham Hill, VRM customer data and competitive advantage,
   28 January 2009 [Online] http://www.customerthink.com/
   blog/vrm_customer_data_and_competitive_advantage.

9 Kim Benjamin, Tesco's not so secret weapon, *Marketing Direct*, 7 June 2007
   [Online] http://www.brandrepublic.com/features/login/662857/.

10 Jenny Davey, Every little bit of data helps Tesco rule retail,
    Sunday Times (London), 4 October 2009.

11 Kim Benjamin, Tesco's not so secret weapon, *Marketing Direct*, 7 June 2007
    [Online] http://www.brandrepublic.com/features/login/662857/.

12 Martin Hayward, *Any Colour You Like as Long as It's Any Colour You Like*,
    Dunnhumby [Online] http://www.dunnhumby.com/admin/files/
    dunnhumby-any-colour-you-like.pdf.

13 Kim Benjamin, Tesco's not so secret weapon, *Marketing Direct*, 7 June 2007
    [Online] http://www.brandrepublic.com/features/login/662857/.

14 Tesco API TJAM – what happened and what's next?, 8 August 2009
    [Online] http://techfortesco.blogspot.com/2009/08/
    tesco-api-tjam-what-happened-and-whats.html.

15 Ibid.

16 Jenny Davey, Every little bit of data helps Tesco rule retail,
    Sunday Times (London), 4 October 2009.

17 Devon Wylie, CRM case study 14, Tesco has links with the corner shops of England's past, 2005 [Online] **http://www.scribd.com/doc/ 43441362/Tesco-CRM-1**.

18 Martin Hayward, *Any Colour You Like as Long as It's Any Colour You Like*, Dunnhumby [Online] **http://www.dunnhumby.com/admin/files/ dunnhumby-any-colour-you-like.pdf**.

The Precision Marketer's Moment

Luck is a matter of preparation meeting opportunity.

SENECA

In this chapter, you will learn:

- about the career of a Precision Marketer and four key paths of Precision Marketing that are emerging;

- how to align marketing objectives across the enterprise:
  - with the CEO;
  - with the CFO;
  - with the CIO;
  - with the COO;
  - with HR;

- how to collaborate to enhance the customer experience.

Precision Marketing is a powerful strategy and approach for marketers, and we believe that this is the Precision Marketer's moment. To make the most of this moment, marketers must be prepared to implement practices vital to this. Precision Marketing represents not only the future of marketing but also the future of business.

In order to create that future, Precision Marketing needs Precision Marketers to apply the principles and approach outlined in this book. Today's marketers – and even aspiring marketers – must step up and provide leadership if this movement is to realize its vast potential. Marketers must take action if they are to experience the business value, contributions and success that now await them on this path.

Precision Marketers' careers

Consider the careers of two marketing visionaries. One left a comfortable professorship at the Harvard Business School to triumph on the Las Vegas Strip, demonstrating that his theories on marketing and customized customer service could deliver enormous pay-offs. The other rose up the ranks at a British retailer, introducing marketing innovations that would, over time, put his firm on top in the United Kingdom and set the stage for global expansion.

We are speaking of Gary Loveman of Caesar's and Terry Leahy of Tesco, respectively. Both men would eventually rise to the role of CEO – a step that few marketers have made in our largest public corporations but one that may become a more common pattern in the coming years. That is because customer-focused and data-driven strategies are now at the heart of success for more and more companies. Precision Marketers, who are actively leveraging customer insight to drive growth to new levels, are in a great position to rise to the top spots of today's enterprises. As we'll show later in the chapter, there is a growing belief that experts in customer intelligence are the cornerstone of value in a corporation, and by default this places Precision Marketers in a strong position to rise to top executive roles in today's organizations if they so desire.

Let's look at the experiences of Gary Loveman and Terry Leahy in greater detail.

The career of Gary Loveman of Caesar's

Loveman, who made his mark in academia with his research on the service economy, originally was intrigued by Caesar's (known then as Harrah's) when he taught postgraduate strategy and marketing courses to some of the company's senior managers. Recognizing an opportunity to apply some of his core ideas, he sent a letter to Harrah's CEO, Phil Satre, providing a few ideas that might contribute to the company's growth. He saw opportunities to unify the company's nationwide mix of casinos and encourage greater customer loyalty across properties. Impressed with his guidance, Satre met Loveman in Atlantic City in January 1998 and offered him the role of Chief Operating Officer, a position that would give him deep insight into the company's marketing operations. Loveman accepted.

Loveman brought an outsider's perspective to the company. Most importantly, he brought a belief that gambling should be treated like retail. Rather than concentrate on high rollers, he believed the company could truly strengthen its profits by focusing on its most frequent customers, including the teachers, machinists and doctors who would return again and again to the company's properties.

Having begun his career running regression models at the Federal Reserve Bank of Boston, and later earning his PhD in economics, Loveman had a gift for analysis and number crunching. He was a popular lecturer at the Harvard Business School and his work on what he calls 'the service–profit chain' contended that there was a direct correlation between company profits, customer loyalty and rewards for the front-line employees most engaged in customer interactions.

Immersing himself in the company's operations, Loveman could see how particular campaigns, incentives and 'service interventions' would influence customer behaviour. Over time, he proved to be an able executive and was tapped to replace Satre when he retired in 2002. One of Loveman's first moves as CEO was to concentrate on growing the spending of existing customers. His key lever was a frequent player's card.

While casinos had always compensated high rollers with luxury suites and free meals, little had been done in the business to earn the loyalty of the many other guests on-property. Loveman believed that loyalty card data could be applied to provide a system of perks, including discounted rooms, express check-in and special seating at the casino's buffets.

By mining these customer data, Caesar's was able to determine its most profitable customers and reward them accordingly. But Caesar's wasn't content to simply reward customers for past behaviour. It also mined its customer data to determine how to drive future behaviour. Caesar's produced customized offers and packages that would entice customers to visit various properties nationwide and would constantly run experiments to learn how best to delight its customers and deepen their loyalty.

This proved to be a powerful means of differentiating the company from other gaming firms better known for their extravagant structures and big-name performers. As Caesar's rose to become the most profitable company in the gaming business, Loveman vividly and handily demonstrated the power of deep customer insight and engagement.[1]

The career of Terry Leahy of Tesco

Half a world away, Terry Leahy was delivering the proof in his own company. It's an opportunity he had waited patiently to seize.

Having joined Tesco in 1979 after graduating from the University of Manchester Institute of Science and Technology, Leahy was promoted to Marketing Manager in 1982. In the mid-1980s he held the position of Marketing Director for Tesco Stores Ltd and later became Commercial Director of Tesco's fresh foods business. In the early 1990s, Leahy was appointed to Tesco's board of directors and become Head of Marketing. And his climb continued. In 1997, at the age of 40, Leahy was named Chief Executive Officer.

It was as head of marketing, however, that Leahy began making some of his boldest moves. In the mid-1990s, retailers throughout the United Kingdom were actively investing in loyalty card programmes. 'Loyalty has emerged as one of the main weapons in the food retailers' endless battle to outdo their rivals,' stated *The Times* in 1995. The major chains – such as Sainsbury's, Safeway and Tesco – launched programmes to make loyalty a driver of profitable growth.

Not all firms, however, remained equally committed to these endeavours. Upon abandoning the programme in 2000, the CEO of Safeway would ultimately describe its programme as a 'backpack of stones' that relied on a 'flashy, worthless piece of plastic.'

Under the leadership of Leahy, Tesco remained proudly committed to its Clubcard loyalty programme. In the mid-1990s the company would begin to outpace market leader Sainsbury's. With 8.5 million card users in 1995, Tesco was collecting data on 400 million shopping baskets, which represented two-thirds of all baskets processed through its registers.

What was most striking about Leahy's approach was that every quarter, following an analysis of the data, the company would mail out relevant and targeted vouchers and coupons to its club members. While other retailers enabled customers to redeem their points at any time at checkout counters, Tesco's approach took loyalty programmes a step further. By sending out customized mailings to millions of customers, Tesco was confronting huge logistical challenges and making significant investments. Each direct mail piece incorporated offers and discounts that were personalized to the recipient based on the customer's purchasing history.

The precise and relevant content of the Clubcard mailings proved to be enormously successful. The company's research demonstrated that customers thought of the quarterly mailings as their personal mail, as opposed to junk mail. Each Tesco mailing generated an impressive sales bump that more than covered the direct mailing cost. In fact, the company claims its mailings have operated at a zero net cost since the programme's launch.

Rich data analysis – drawn from the Clubcard data – proved to be the true secret weapon underlying Leahy's strategy. This analysis enabled Tesco to identify new opportunities based on the customer's lifestyle or life stage. Segmentation analysis even helped the company identify the 20 per cent of customers who represented 80 per cent of revenues and profits – and take steps to lock in their loyalty. The data also allowed Tesco to move into new businesses, such as online shopping and financial services, that reflected the preferences and priorities of its customer base.

Knighted in 2002, Sir Terry recently retired as CEO of Tesco. He left the company in the leading position in the UK market, poised to stretch its wings globally. The company is now operating in 14 nations worldwide.

As Leahy puts it, the company's commitment to its customers has been a key factor in its success and an incredibly powerful aspect of Tesco's culture. 'The workers have to believe in the business for reasons other than remuneration,' he says. 'A relationship with customers has to be from the foundation up; customers are the start, not the end of the business.'[2]

So what sets both Loveman and Leahy apart? Clearly, one key factor is their commitment to mining customer insight and intelligence to drive new business strategies. Through their solid leadership and dynamic, disciplined and analytically inclined efforts, Loveman and Leahy have demonstrated and proved the power of Precision Marketing in today's world economy and set the stage for a new customer-focused future.

Alignment at the heart of the Chief Marketing Officer's success

While Loveman and Leahy certainly represent compelling examples of the potential ahead for precision marketers, it's critical to recognize that, to date, most chief marketing officers are failing to accomplish anything close to what these men accomplished.

In its 2009 report on CMO tenure, executive search firm Spencer Stuart found that the average CMO at major firms is just 34.7 months. While this figure was about 13 months higher than average CMO tenures in 2004, it still suggests that individuals in top marketing roles are exceedingly vulnerable.[3]

When the firm studied the traits of the most successful CMOs, one interesting finding was the critical role of alignment with other members of the executive team in achieving marketing success. According to Spencer Stuart:

> Based on our experience, the most common cause for such marketing tenures is grounded principally in expectations – both from the perspective of the CEO as well as the peer group to the CMO. If these executives do not share similar expectations of the marketing organization with the CMO, chances for CMO failure are increased. And when there is the added pressure from shareholders, the media and boards of directors for nearly instantaneous results, the differences in expectations can cause major strife within the organization.[4]

Alignment across functional areas is central to the CMO's success – and even more so to the Precision Marketer's success – so they must quickly become experts at executive bridge-building or ensuring alignment with other key leaders and groups in the enterprise. According to Joseph Tripodi, CMO at Coca-Cola:

> A CMO is not an island. There has to be a clear understanding of the role of marketing within the organization and it has to be articulated. CMOs have to build bridges to other parts of the organization to enable shared success. Marketing is definitely an important part of a company, but it's only one part.[5]

Whether you are a CMO, you report to one, or you are someone simply trying to execute a customer-focused strategy, it's clear that your success will depend on solid alignment and collaboration. This may be Precision Marketing's moment, but it won't be truly seized unless you are prepared to implement the strategies and tactics that are vital to this approach and make this the Precision Marketer's moment.

Engaging the enterprise

To be effective in their efforts to establish alignment, marketing executives must consider and comprehend the perspectives of various individuals and groups. Through their understanding of these many perspectives, they can become not only more successful at internal alignment but aligned with the market and customer as well. The CMO's peers, after all, play roles that will contribute, in one way or another, to the customer's experience.

So how might you and your team members go about winning support for your ongoing endeavours with various executives and groups? Consider the different parties that must be engaged:

Engaging the CEO

No one is more essential to the CMO's success than the CEO. The CMO is responsible for embracing the CEO's agenda and carrying it forward to the marketplace. The CEO also sets the strategic objectives against which marketing will be measured and assessed.

The challenge the CMO faces lies in translating the CEO's high-level strategic objectives into the tactical and operational actions that will meet them. The highest agenda item, many times, is growth, whether it is defined in terms of overall revenue, market share or wallet share. Precision Marketers have a valuable opportunity in this sense. By demonstrating that their methods represent a superior and more enduring path to growth than conventional marketing strategies, they can earn the confidence of the CEO.

Marketing is not merely executing the CEO's strategy, however. The CEO is also looking for a report on market trends and opportunities, and customer insight is essential. According to Bob Harris, President of the LendingTree Exchange and its former CMO:

> The buck stops with the CEO. However, the marketing leader should be part of the CEO's inner circle, with a strong voice and sense of responsibility for the knowledge and input required to make key strategic decisions based on customer insights. In the end, marketers should see the big growth opportunities sooner than the rest of the organization, including the CEO, with an eye on what the company should do to be relevant in the future.[6]

Engaging the CFO

While the CMO's relationship with the chief financial officer is critical, it is a relationship that is vulnerable to mismanagement. The main problem is that these executives – and their respective groups – tend to speak different languages. Finance executives are relying on marketing to drive shareholder value, predictable cash flows and steady revenue growth. They don't have much interest in awareness or lead metrics. Campaign performance doesn't interest them as much as bottom-line performance.

Marketing, however, needs finance on its side. Not only is the CFO's support necessary to fund new marketing initiatives, but the CFO's evaluation of marketing's performance will heavily influence the perceptions of other executives in the C-suite. According to the Marketing Leadership Council, top-performing marketing organizations tend to have a strong relationship with the finance groups. If finance is to be a top supporter of Precision Marketing initiatives and the budgets necessary to conduct them, the CMO must make a consistent effort to remain aligned with the CFO.

Through an open and vigorous dialogue, CMOs and CFOs can develop common performance frameworks to address some of the most important challenges facing their enterprises. One particular opportunity lies in working together to better understand what drives intangible value. Says Brian McCarthy, a senior executive in Accenture's finance and performance management service line:

> [W]hether it's around the brand or customer acquisition or retention or loyalty, they need to understand which of those factors are important to driving the overall financial performance of the company.
>
> And then they need to put in place rigorous performance management and analytics to help them understand what's actually driving specific outcomes at a much more actionable level. The interface between the CMO and the CFO is in terms of performance management and analytics – how you make investments in these intangible assets, how you see the return on them, how you measure them – and in understanding how they will impact the bottom line.[7]

Engaging the CIO

Precision Marketing is highly dependent on the ability to fully leverage information technology. The digitization of marketing and customer communications means that the CMO and CIO (Chief Information Officer) must become increasingly collaborative to be successful.

A recent study conducted by the CMO Council found that CMO success is highly correlated to the successful bridging of the gap across functional and organizational silos – most significantly, between marketing and IT. The study found that CIOs and CMOs agree on the top three drivers for greater alignment between their two organizations, which are shown in Figure 10.1.[8]

FIGURE 10.1 Drivers of CIO-CMO Alignment

Three drivers of CIO–CMO alignment	Who says?	
	CIO	CMO
1. Technology now underpins entire customer experience	65%	50%
2. Access to customer intelligence critical to competitive advantage	53%	55%
3. Reaching and engaging the market has become more digitally driven	40%	44%

SOURCE: Adapted from CMO Council, *The CMO–CIO Alignment Imperative: Driving revenue through customer relevance*, October 2010.

However, while there are these three key areas of agreement, the report highlights the fact that there are some notable areas of disagreement between the CMO and CIO. Understanding these gaps is critical to spanning the silos between functional areas. Specifically, the report highlights that

> Both sides agree the top area of CIO focus should be the delivery of more timely and relevant transactional, behavioral and customer insight data. But on the IT side, there is a stronger focus on automating customer interactions and handling and furthering the use of social media for online listening. Marketing, on the other hand, believes IT should first focus on improving linkages between functional marketing, sales and channel groups and on the deployment of better marketing execution platforms and operational systems. Both sides are focused on important issues, but they need to come together in strategizing and prioritizing projects.[9]

According to the same report, CMOs are

> at the helm of global marketing organizations that are increasingly technology, mobility, connectivity and digitally driven. Protection of the customer experience, heightened sensitivity to security issues around customer privacy and data, and the automated management of brand assets, customer insights and automated marketing supply chains and operational systems are increasing the demand for robust back-office and IT infrastructures.[10]

To execute today's customer- and data-driven strategies, CMOs and CIOs must be deeply aligned and collaborative. 'Companies that fail to align their marketing and technology functions will quickly be bested by those that harness the two, engaging customers with relevant information and offers, encouraging long-term dialogue and deeper relationships,' states the CMO Council. 'In the end, the ultimate objective must be to achieve a state of absolute customer relevance; a state of being that makes brands robust, resilient and highly valued in the market.'[11]

Engaging the COO

A company will waste its investment in relevant messages if the company cannot fulfil the demand created by Precision Marketing activities. For example, there is no point in the company promoting a product if that product is not on the shelf when the customer gets to the store. Companies gain added revenues from Precision Marketing by predicting customer response, and the role of the chief operating officer (COO) is to prepare the organization to deliver to that response.

Tesco illustrates some of the integration issues between marketing and operations. Tesco in fact uses its data on customers to improve many aspects of operations, such as merchandising, on-shelf availability, pricing, the format of its stores and even where to locate its stores. Tesco's Clubcard data help the company decide what products to put on store shelves. For example, Tesco introduced Asian herbs to its stores in neighbourhoods where high concentrations of Indian and Pakistani customers lived. Clubcard data quickly showed that affluent white customers liked the exotic herbs, too. So Tesco rolled out the new products more broadly.[12] Tesco also launched a series of differentiated store brands that aligned with the customer segments uncovered in the Clubcard data. These five newly identified customer segments include segments that Tesco calls Tesco Value, Tesco Finest, Tesco Organic, Tesco Fair Trade and Tesco Free From.[13]

Tesco even used its customer data to fend off cut-price competitors. Wal-Mart owns Asda and competes with Tesco using Wal-Mart's ruthless price-cutting strategy. Tesco knows that some of its customers are price-sensitive and might defect to Asda's ultra-low prices. Yet Tesco doesn't want to cut prices too much and lose too much profit. Tesco used its Clubcard data to identify who among its customers were the most price-sensitive and what items those price-sensitive buyers bought most often. Tesco discovered that cost-conscious consumers bought its Tesco Value own-brand margarine regularly. So Tesco lowered the price of that margarine, along with other items most often bought in conjunction with the margarine. As a result, shoppers didn't defect to Asda. In fact, Tesco sales jumped 17 per cent. 'Tesco has become the first organization to use customer insight to actually run its business well. In the past, people just used customer data to make their marketing more effective,' says Clive Humby of Dunnhumby.[14]

Most of all, companies can learn whether their messaging and products are the right ones by listening to the messages that customers send to the company. The most important message from customers is buying behaviour. Sir Terry Leahy explains that 'each transaction, each bleep at the checkout, is a message to a business to produce more of that product – and helps to shape a trend. Find a business that responds to those signals, and you have found a successful company'.[15]

Engaging product development and innovation

Companies can also use the data, analytics and strategies of Precision Marketing to grow the company overall. For example, once a company knows its customers and engages with those customers, it can offer a broader range of products and services. The company can develop or offer new products that its customers will be more likely to buy. For instance, Amazon.com started as an online bookstore, but the company's core competence in predictive analytics on what people want to buy based on what they've bought before or looked at before let the company expand into movies, consumer electronics, toys, home products and so forth. Similarly, Clubcard data helped Tesco expand from groceries into electronics, clothing, mobile phones, banking and more.

By engaging more with its customers, a company can learn about their unmet needs, which then provides a focus for innovation and product development. For example, Collette Vacations offers nearly 200 tours to a wide range of destinations and adds about a dozen new options per year. By analysing web traffic, online customer behaviour and internet marketing initiatives, Collette can gauge interest in potential new offerings even before any customer has bought a single tour. Patterns of engagement let Collette understand what people are most interested in and then Collette can develop new tours to match.

Similarly, customers of B2B companies want more say in innovation. A survey of B2B technology companies and their customers found that 6 out of 10 customers say that co-innovation is extremely or very important.[16] France Telecom went so far as to merge its marketing and innovation departments. To the extent that Precision Marketing means understanding what customers want, Precision Marketing insights can play a valuable role in new product development and innovation.

Engaging HR

The same Precision Marketing Framework that helps companies engage with customers can be used to help engage with employees. Creating better relationships and understanding behaviours applies to both customers and employees. Given the labour costs of reading messages, a company will want a precision messaging strategy so that no employee spends work time reading irrelevant messages. Precision messages to employees help those employees do their jobs better.

In the case of human relations applications of Precision Marketing Framework concepts, the objectives might be:

- cost reductions;
- productivity improvements;
- employee retention; or
- better compliance with company guidelines.

The data that the company could use include employee activities, performance and demographics. The principles of rules-based segmentation and predictive analytics can be used for opportunities to say the right thing to the right employee to get the right outcome without blasting all employees with imprecise messages. Deployment through internal and external communications channels (eg newsletters, e-mail, SMS, etc) can lead to measurable changes in employee behaviour.

For example, we and our colleagues at Ricoh worked with Sinclair on the fuel company's 'Fleet Track', which is Sinclair's premier commercial fleet fuelling card programme.[17] The programme included a precision messaging campaign that helps fleet operators communicate with their truck-driving employees while on the road. Sinclair set up consolidated, real-time capture of all of the relevant data when truckers refuel, purchase food or make other business-related expenditures. When drivers make a purchase, they get immediate point-of-purchase feedback with messages that indicate they have reached their daily limit for food expenditures. Alternatively, the message might thank them for filling up at point A but let them know they could have saved a certain dollar amount by filling up at point B.

The benefits for drivers are that it will be easier to manage expenses and optimize their day. In turn, the company will benefit by reducing costs using this system. Sinclair used MAPPING Suite, a complete, customized multichannel business communication software system that brings together document databases, design, composition, analytics and multichannel distribution. The system lets companies deliver timely messages to the right person.

Precision Marketing techniques can also be used in HR benefits administration. For example, Tesco won the 'Communications Strategy of the Year' award at the Employee Benefits Awards 2009 by creating an individualized total reward statement for each employee that provided lucid information and illustrations.[18] The award judges noted that Tesco 'proved communication can be done simply, cheaply and comprehensively, with messages drip-fed through as many channels as possible.'[19] The same ethos of Precision Marketing and response testing that Tesco uses to promote green beans to millions of consumers can be used to market the company's employee benefits programmes to its 440,000 employees.

Keys to alignment

To earn the trust and confidence of executives throughout the enterprise, marketers must take the time to reach out to them and begin seeing the business through their eyes.

In an era of Precision Marketing, the success of the marketing organization hinges on alignment with the rest of the enterprise. The marketing team simply cannot act alone. It needs the understanding, support and collaboration of the CEO, the CFO, the CIO, the sales organization and the channel managers, as well as many other groups, if it is to perform effectively.

The key to credibility is recognizing the special and essential asset that marketing will bring to these various groups: customer insight. In fact, Precision Marketing puts your customers at the centre of all marketing and then evolves to make your customers the centre of your entire business. This point is made clear by this comment from Mohanbir S Sawhney, an influential marketing professor with the Kellogg School of Management:

> Marketers often complain about the lack of authority and lack of influence over their colleagues in engineering, operations or finance. The simple fact is – nobody will give you a seat at the table; you have to earn it. And the best way to gain power is through knowing your customers better than anyone else in the organization.[20]

How can marketing drive organizational alignment and strengthen its own credibility? Here are a few core factors that will contribute to alignment:

- *Valuable insights*. This factor revolves around the marketer's ability to rigorously analyse and make sense of relevant customer and market trends. Whether quantitative or qualitative, these insights are valued among other executives who are intent on planning and investing to meet their own particular objectives. Data-driven marketers can use their unique insights to deepen bonds with their colleagues.

- *Reliable guidance.* Once market and customer insights have been generated, they must be communicated and made actionable. Other executives will look to marketing for guidance as to where markets are headed and what trends represent significant opportunities (as well as avoidable risks). By having a finger on the pulse of the market, you have an opportunity to become a trusted adviser. However, you must speak the language of the party you are intent on engaging. Learning the language of various constituent groups takes time, effort and care, and, most importantly, it takes data-driven insights.

- *Consistent engagement.* Successful marketers are boundary spanners. They avoid getting wrapped up in silos. To build continuing support for their marketing strategies, they recognize that they must continuously cross silos and organizational barriers to develop relationships. They recognize that their leadership must be based on persuasion and influence as opposed to status or coercion. By engaging peers and colleagues on a consistent basis, through meetings and forums of varying kinds, you too can learn what it takes to win their trust and confidence.

With deep insight into the customer, marketing truly is in a unique and powerful position. Precision Marketers are particularly well placed to add real, measurable value to the business. They build skills, capabilities and assets that increasingly drive profitability throughout the enterprise. By providing advice and guidance to their colleagues, they can help them match their actions to the real dynamics of a customer-driven marketplace. That's a powerful value proposition – one that will expand skills and generate results while it also opens doors by building bridges with other executives.

Southwest Airlines is one company that focused on ensuring the consistency of the customer experience across channels and embedding a commitment to customer satisfaction in its culture. Dave Ridley, its Senior Vice President of Marketing, states, 'We are a marketing-driven company in the sense that all of us, from operations to customer service agents at the ticket counter to headquarters, are sensitive and listen to our customers' wants and needs.'[21]

It is the role of the Precision Marketer to bring the 'voice of the customer' into the enterprise and to help make the customer the centre of the business across all functions. By actively collaborating with all the groups that directly touch the customer, marketing can both take the steps to ensure that it is hearing that voice and then act to ensure that the customer's experience is expertly managed.

Collaborating to enhance the customer experience

Of course, there are many executives and groups that top marketers must engage with to establish credibility and deliver strong results. The array of relationships that are most critical and deserve the most attention will depend on the nature of the enterprise. But the set of relationships that CMOs engaged in Precision Marketing approaches certainly must cultivate are those that are most directly and intimately related to the customer's experience.

We speak here of relationships with chief sales officers, executives managing touchpoints (such as the website and contact centre) and those managing partner channels (where the enterprise's relationship with the customer may be indirect). The success of Precision Marketing revolves around customer interaction in many channels and touchpoints. Should the customer's experience prove disappointing or inconsistent in any sphere, it threatens to undermine the work of marketing to acquire new customers, build loyalty and drive growth. Should retention rates drop or growth rates stall, marketing organizations will prove exceedingly vulnerable, whether or not customer disappointments and defections are within their immediate control.

However, the marketing organization's intimate customer and market knowledge can help other groups within the enterprise influence the customer experience. This knowledge should play to everyone's benefit. Of course, there may be conflicts. Contact centre managers, for instance, are sometimes pressured to cut calls short or keep customers on hold to save money rather than hire more customer service representatives. E-commerce managers may be pressured to shower customers with inappropriate offers in order to make some ill-considered quota. This is where marketing can play a valuable role by balancing short-term imperatives with insights into customer value and perspectives on the long-term value of customer relationships.

The next-generation CMO

Forrester Research contends that companies will soon 'elevate customer intelligence within their organizations and use it as a competitive weapon.' Consequently, the research firm believes the 'next generation' of CMOs will come from roles in which the management and analysis of customer data is central to marketing performance. It says:

> Today, customer intelligence executives enable organizations to successfully manage relationships with highly empowered customers who have a dwindling tolerance for marketing. Tomorrow, they will create customer intelligence command centers to drive competitive strategy and create competitive advantage.[22]

In its survey of hundreds of companies, Forrester found that most firms today have a customer intelligence function. Corporate respondents said they have groups devoted to such areas as marketing analytics (80 per cent), customer feedback (78 per cent) and database marketing (75 per cent). Only 30 per cent of respondents claimed that the customer intelligence group is enterprise-wide (Figure 10.2).[23]

FIGURE 10.2 Forrester Study

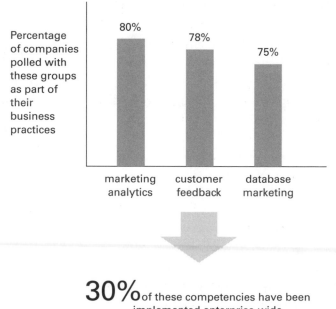

Percentage of companies polled with these groups as part of their business practices

80%   78%   75%

marketing analytics   customer feedback   database marketing

30% of these competencies have been implemented enterprise-wide

As the role matures within organizations, Forrester expects customer intelligence to become a 'command center for the business – serving up actionable information as the fuel that drives multichannel customer communications, product development, strategic planning, and even operations'.[24] Clearly, this movement is essential to the rise of Precision Marketing.

Career paths for Precision Marketers

As Forrester Research suggests, there are a number of interesting career paths for individuals who hope to succeed as Precision Marketers. Forrester identifies four key roles that are now emerging:

- *Marketing technologists*. These individuals tend to be individuals with a background in database marketing, marketing operations or IT. They are responsible for managing and coordinating marketing IT investments. As their roles evolve to include new listening platforms, online communities and web analytics, they are expected to come into contact with a widening set of business partners. This represents an opportunity to identify and learn some of the most important levers of performance going forward.

- *Marketing scientists*. These individuals tend to be specialists in advanced mathematics, quantitative analysis or research. They deploy analytics and modelling to turn customer data into actionable insight. As they learn to speak the language of business, their knowledge of numbers will serve them particularly well. Demand for their ability to analyse trends and identify opportunities will only grow in the coming years.

- *Marketing practitioners*. These individuals tend to have backgrounds in direct marketing, interactive marketing or production and fulfilment. They manage campaign execution across channels. Their skills are expected to become increasingly valued as the channel complexity further increases and interactive marketing becomes more pervasive. Their background in rigorous, direct marketing approaches – such as test and learn – will soon be valued on a wider scale.

- *Customer strategists*. These individuals tend to come from marketing technology, marketing science, marketing operations or strategy consulting. They are responsible for driving enterprise-wide adoption of customer intelligence as an asset. They are expected to become some of the primary catalysts and evangelists for this approach, enabling groups throughout the business to see how actionable insight will enhance the customer experience and drive growth.[25]

This may not prove to be an exhaustive list for individuals who are seeking opportunities to propel their careers on a foundation of Precision Marketing. We expect many of tomorrow's top Precision Marketers to come from other areas of the organization. We envision marketing leaders who emerge from operational roles or various customer-facing backgrounds. Some top marketers may have long tenures at their companies (like Terry Leahy), move around between companies or come from an entirely different field (like Gary Loveman).

Whatever the path you choose, it is important to understand the importance of Precision Marketing and how this movement will influence the trajectory of business overall. What seems clear is that companies are becoming increasingly customer focused as opposed to product focused. In order to successfully adopt this strategy (or make this transition), they will need to know their customers intimately and actively capitalize on this knowledge.

Revolutionary leaders for revolutionary times

'With the number of airline-issued credit cards, grocery-store club cards, department-store credit cards, and reward accounts with hotels, airlines, and car-rental agencies, companies have tons of information about their customers and their purchase patterns,' argues Jeffrey Pfeffer, a professor at the Stanford Graduate School of Business. 'But almost no companies use that data strategically.'[26] Caesar's and Tesco are obviously two notable exceptions to Pfeffer's statement. They are not alone. Companies such as ING, Amazon and CapitalOne – firms we have featured in this book – are demonstrating the growing power and potential of turning insight into relevance. They are growth leaders on the new frontier of business.

Executive leaders, marketers and other customer-facing professionals who grasp these trends are in a tremendous position to catapult both their companies and their careers to new levels. If you believe that business success will increasingly revolve around engaging customers on a more personal level, you'll want to embrace the revolution in relevance that is now under way. It is time to seize the Precision Marketer's moment.

Key takeaway messages from Chapter 10,
'The Precision Marketer's Moment'

- The four key roles emerging for Precision Marketer careers are those of marketing technologists, marketing scientists, marketing practitioners and customer strategists.

- To align with the CEO, translate the CEO's high-level strategic objectives into tactical and operational actions that will meet the objectives.

- Align with the CFO by speaking the language of finance. Don't talk about 'impressions' and 'click-throughs'. Instead, show how marketing is improving the bottom line. Focus on how marketing is helping to drive shareholder value, predictable cash flows and steady revenue growth.

- Engage with the CIO and collaborate closely, because Precision Marketing is highly dependent on the ability to fully leverage information technology. This includes working together to prioritize projects and deploy marketing execution platforms.

- Communicate often with the COO to ensure that if marketing drives customers to buy, the products and services will be there when they are needed. There's no point in promoting a product if it's not available when the customer wants to buy it.

- Use the six steps of the Precision Marketing Framework to better engage with employees, not just customers. Use the Precision Marketing Framework to create relevant, timely messages to employees.

- Enhance the customer experience by maintaining good relations with the Chief Sales Officer and managers at all customer touchpoints (such as the website and contact centre) and those managing partner channels (where the enterprise's relationship with the customer may be indirect). The success of Precision Marketing revolves around customer interaction in many channels and touchpoints. Should the customer's experience prove disappointing or inconsistent in any sphere, it threatens to undermine the work of marketing to acquire new customers, build loyalty and drive growth.

Notes

1   http://www.caesars.com/corporate/index.html.

2   Global Corporate Achievement Awards, Leadership built on experience: an interview with Sir Terry Leahy, 2002 [Online] **http://www.eiu.com/ site_info.asp?info_name=AwardsSir_Terry_Leahy_interview&entry1= AwardsNav1&infositelayout=site_info_nav_awards&rf=0**.

3 Spencer Stuart, CMO Tenure: Slowing down the revolving door, 2010 [Online] **http://www.the-cma.org/?WCE=C=47|K=229856**.

4 Spencer Stuart, CMO Tenure: Slowing down the revolving door, 2004 [Online] **http://content.spencerstuart.com/sswebsite/pdf/lib/CMO_brochureU1.pdf**.

5 Ibid.

6 Scott M. Davis, *The Shift: The transformation of today's marketers into tomorrow's growth leaders*, John Wiley, New York, 2009, p 41.

7 John Cummings, CFO, meet your CMO (you'll be glad you did), *Business Finance*, 22 February 2008.

8 CMO Council, *The CMO–CIO Alignment Imperative: Driving revenue through customer relevance*, 2010.

9 Ibid.

10 Ibid.

11 Ibid.

12 Cecile Rohwedder, Stores of knowledge: No. 1 retailer in Britain uses 'Clubcard' to thwart Wal-Mart, *Wall Street Journal*, 6 June 2006.

13 Coriolis Research, Tesco: A case study in supermarket excellence, July 2004 [Online] **http://www.coriolisresearch.com/pdfs/coriolis_tesco_study_in_excellence.pdf**.

14 Loyalty Square, Tesco: Every little helps [Online] **http://loyaltysquare.com/tesco.php**.

15 Nick Webster, Sir Terry Leahy planning Tesco's way out of recession, 12 June 2009 [Online] **http://www.clickliverpool.com/business/corporate-news/124772-sir-terry-leahy-planning-tescos-way-out-of-recession.html**.

16 CMO Council, 'Customer affinity' new measure of B2B marketing effectiveness [Online] **http://www.marketingcharts.com/direct/cmo-council-customer-affinity-new-measure-of-b2b-marketing-effectiveness-2765/cmo-council-customer-centricity-of-vendor-communityjpg/**.

17 Another score for InfoPrint: But is it TransPromo or TransInfo? [Online] **http://toughloveforxerox.blogspot.com/2009/08/another-score-for-infoprint-but-is-it.html**.

18 Employee Benefits Awards 2009, Communications strategy of the year for organisations with 5,000 employees or more [Online] **http://www.employeebenefits.co.uk/cgi-bin/item.cgi?ap=1&id=9054**.

19 Ibid.

20 Mohanbir Sawhney, A manifesto for marketing, *CMO* magazine, September 2004 [Online] **http://magnostic.wordpress.com/ best-of-cmo/a-manifesto-for-marketing/**.

21 Daniel Mccarthy, CMO Council explores customer experience in difficult market, *B2B*, 13 October 2008 [Online] **http://www.btobonline.com/ apps/pbcs.dll/article?AID=/20081013/FREE/310139976/1109/FREE**.

22 Dave Frankland, The intelligent approach to customer intelligence, Forrester Research, 16 October 2009 [Online] **http://www.forrester.com/ rb/Research/intelligent_approach_to_customer_intelligence/q/ id/55051/t/2**

23 Ibid.

24 SAS Institute, Turning customer data into analytical marketing fuel: how to use analytically driven customer insight for extraordinary competitive advantage, 2010 [Online] **http://www.sas.com/resources/whitepaper/ wp_20338.pdf**.

25 Ibid.

26 Jeffrey Pfeffer, Information is a strategic resource, so use it, *CBS Money Watch*, 4 May 2009 [Online] **http://www.bnet.com/blog/business-psychology/ information-is-a-strategic-resource-so-use-it/182**.

Conclusion
Your Moment

> *And the trouble is, if you don't risk anything, you risk even more.*
>
> **ERICA JONG**

Let's fast-forward in time. Imagine that you are able to use the clarifying perspective of hindsight to look back at your professional contributions and personal achievements. What do you want your legacy to look like?

The benefit of hindsight has shown that as people mature and age, it becomes increasingly important to achieve significance vs pure monetary success. Knowing that we added value and made a difference in this world is what we all truly hunger for and is something that we continually strive to achieve. Significance, it seems, is ever elusive.

As marketers, we believe that this is our moment. Our fork in the road. Our moment to choose

We believe that the climate will become increasingly challenging for conventional marketers. Your organization's success – and your personal success as a marketer – will depend on taking new directions. You must confront the status quo and take some chances. New marketing initiatives can seem overwhelming. Change can be exceedingly difficult. In fact, this is the point at which many potential catalysts – change agents – become paralyzed.

We have shown you in a myriad of real-world examples, across industries and geographies and businesses, where Precision Marketing is the marketing enabler to bring more value to your business. If the path to adopt Precision Marketing was easy, many more companies would have 'flipped the switch' and moved forward. Implementing Precision Marketing requires courage. It is complex. It is sophisticated. It is not easy. It requires commitment. It requires dedication. It requires perseverance. It is a journey. And it is totally worth it. In the words of Erica Jong, 'And... the trouble is, if you don't risk anything, you risk even more.'

With risk comes potential pay-off. There are few inflection points in your career that represent the magnitude of pay-off that we believe Precision Marketing can provide – to your business, to your growth, to you and to the significance you can create. We believe that this is your moment.

The business process of precision

Precision Marketing is an ongoing business process. Knowing customers and creating relevance isn't a one-time event, it's an ongoing activity because:

- customers needs change;
- your company gains new customers;
- customers go through various phases of their relationship with your company;
- your company adds new products and services;
- technology provides new touchpoints.

It is our view that the future of marketing – and business – will revolve around deeper customer engagement. We are in the midst of a dramatic marketing transformation. Considering the growing demands and expectations of today's consumers, it is increasingly clear that enterprises must provide an exceptional experience to win and thrive in the coming years.

The reality is that many others will fail to take this journey. They will remain trapped in the approaches that have played well in the past. They will be unable – or unwilling – to explore a new path that leads them to Precision Marketing. They may even buy into the view that customers simply want low-priced products as opposed to a personalized experience. They may miss this opportunity to generate significance in their business, their career, their world.

This is the moment to play smart and play well. Investing now will reap future rewards. What today's customers now ask of us is something different from what they asked of us in the past. Customers no longer expect us to merely respond. They want us to anticipate. They want us to envision what will help them achieve greater success or a more powerful experience. They want suppliers and service providers who know them intimately and can provide offers, products and services that match their personal needs. Customers want to be treated as individuals.

Some might wonder: but wouldn't the customer just turn off all marketing messages? The answer is an emphatic 'no!'. Just look at the fact that customers do opt in, do register to get information about products, do open some e-mails and do respond to some direct mail. Why do some company's TV ads go viral on YouTube? Why does Tesco get millions of more people joining its loyalty programme when those people know full well it means getting more mail and messages from Tesco? It's because some companies know that if you deliver a meaningful, rewarding, timely, entertaining and informative message to the customer, then people will gladly accept it. Not only will consumers listen to your messages, but they will give you their private data and creative energies to help you become more relevant to them

Yet you won't be able to meet an individual's objectives unless you have insight. You have to richly understand your customers and what they value most. How will you do this?

As we have seen, the companies that are now transforming markets – companies like Caesar's, Tesco and Amazon – know their customers intimately. They are the vanguard of the Precision Marketing movement. These leading companies anticipate their customer's next moves and know how – and when – to make an offer that a customer will value. You get to this point of precision by having superior customer insight and the ability to act on it.

These top performers collect customer data, they analyse those data and then they rely on the data to take action. They make the journey from Step One through to Step Six – and then come full circle again. They are intent on reaching their customers with a relevant message and then providing them a truly relevant solution. That's how they roll.

We hope that you will not be intimidated by the demands of the Precision Marketing journey. You can start exactly where you are. That's the key. The most difficult step is the first one. And the rewards will be well worth the journey. As Thomas Edison said, 'If we did the things we are capable of, we would astound ourselves.'

Now it's time to consider the present. Where are you now? Are you prepared to embark upon a journey? Are you willing to conquer the marketing transformation that can lead to new levels of significance? Will you take the first step?

We encourage you to make your move – and seize your moment.

New Horizons

Unless you are willing

to launch out far from

sight of the shore

into the deep beyond

your present comfort zone,

you will never know

what you are capable

of doing or becoming,

nor will you ever discover

the new horizons

and greater dreams

your heart

is yearning for.

Dick Innes

© Copyright 2000
Used by permission of Dick Innes

INDEX

NB: page numbers in *italic* indicate figures or tables